What people are saying about …

FAITHFUL
with
MUCH

"*Faithful with Much* is a moving testimony from two of my friends Tony and Carin Amaradio. Tony and Carin share how they've learned to use their resources for God's glory. Their story illustrates that everything you own is only on loan from God. Reading this book will inspire and challenge you to live generously."

Rick Warren, senior pastor of Saddleback Church and author of *A Purpose Driven Life*

"In *Faithful with Much,* my friends Tony and Carin share the testimony of two generous givers. They have been entrusted with wealth, and through a careful study of Scripture, they have learned how God wants them (and all of His people) to use those resources for His eternal purpose. In this easy-to-read but excellent book, the Amaradios show how we can best use our resources to advance the kingdom of God."

Chuck Colson, founder of Prison Fellowship

"Serving God wisely simply means being a good steward of the time, talents, and treasure He gives us, and I'm grateful to my friends Tony and Carin Amaradio for honing down the most important principles of godly stewardship into their new book, *Faithful with*

Much. Truly, these friends back up their wisdom with a wealth of kingdom-works. They are serving God *wisely!"*

Joni Eareckson Tada, founder of Joni and
Friends International Disability Center

"What a great expression of God's grace at work in and through His servants! The integration of professional financial management and generous stewardship reflected by Tony and Carin encourages each of us to explore the boundaries of our own faith and stewardship."

Dr. Bruce Smith, president of Wycliffe Associates

"*Faithful with Much* is more than the title of this book—it is a perfect description of the way Tony and Carin Amaradio live their lives. Their unique blend of personal transparency and passion for Jesus Christ overflows on every page. This book will open your eyes, quicken your heart, and bless your life as you learn to be faithful with whatever God has entrusted to you."

Gregg Harris, president of Far East Broadcasting Company

"The model of biblical stewardship that Tony and Carin describe in this book—and more importantly, live out in their lives—is a much-needed prescription for the whole of the Christian movement in North America. What they write about is not just theory. It is wise, street-level generosity with enormous kingdom results."

Dr. Sam Metcalf, president of Church Resource Ministries US

"With dramatic stories of their own journey in discovering everything we have truly belongs to the Lord, wealth-management experts Tony and Carin Amaradio offer solid, biblical principles to understand our responsibilities to be wise stewards of the financial gifts with which God has blessed us. Take time to read this book; it could be the best investment you ever make."

Les Steckel, veteran NFL coach, president of the Fellowship of Christian Athletes, and author of *One Yard Short*

"Tony and Carin Amaradio have written a truly powerful testimony of how God can use our resources to maximize His kingdom. They make an often murky and confusing subject—our financial stewardship—clear and convicting. This book is a true blessing to the kingdom.

Dr. Carl A. Moeller, president and CEO of Open Doors USA

"Money is such an important topic in the Bible that it is the main subject of nearly half of Jesus' parables. There is a fundamental connection between our spiritual lives and how we think about and handle money. That is why this new book *Faithful with Much*, written by Tony and Carin Amaradio, is so very timely. Tony and Carin speak from practical experience on how to live a balanced and obedient life for Jesus Christ in all areas, including our finances. Few could have done it with the wisdom, passion, and life experience of the Amaradios. This book could change your way of thinking on this vital topic, and I recommend it to you."

Greg Laurie, pastor of Harvest Christian Fellowship and author of *The Upside-Down Church*

FAITHFUL
with
MUCH

FAITHFUL

with

MUCH

Breaking down the Barriers to Generous Giving

TONY AND CARIN
AMARADIO

FAITHFUL WITH MUCH
Published by David C. Cook
4050 Lee Vance View
Colorado Springs, CO 80918 U.S.A.

David C. Cook Distribution Canada
55 Woodslee Avenue, Paris, Ontario, Canada N3L 3E5

David C. Cook U.K., Kingsway Communications
Eastbourne, East Sussex BN23 6NT, England

David C. Cook and the graphic circle C logo
are registered trademarks of Cook Communications Ministries.

The Web site addresses recommended throughout this book are offered as a resource
to you. These Web sites are not intended in any way to be or imply an endorsement
on the part of David C. Cook, nor do we vouch for their content.

All Scripture quotations, unless otherwise noted, are taken from the *Holy Bible, New International Version®. NIV®.* Copyright © 1973, 1978, 1984 by International Bible Society. Used by permission of Zondervan. All rights reserved. Scripture quotations marked NKJV are taken from the New King James Version. Copyright © 1982 by Thomas Nelson, Inc. Used by permission. All rights reserved. Scripture quotations marked ESV are taken from *The Holy Bible, English Standard Version.* Copyright © 2000; 2001 by Crossway Bibles, a division of Good News Publishers. Used by permission. All rights reserved. Scripture quotations marked NASB are taken from the *New American Standard Bible,* © Copyright 1960, 1995 by The Lockman Foundation. Used by permission

LCCN 2008938850
ISBN 978-0-7814-0484-6
eISBN 978-1-4347-0234-0

© 2009 Tony and Carin Amaradio

The Team: Dan Rich, Steve Parolini, Jaci Schneider, and Karen Athen
Cover Design: Amy Kiechlin
Cover Photos: © iStock
Printed in the United States of America
First Edition 2009

1 2 3 4 5 6 7 8 9 10

042310

Then He said to them, "Beware, and be on your guard against every form of greed; for not even when one has an abundance does his life consist of his possessions."

—*Luke 12:15* NASB

*To our children, grandchildren, and the generations
to follow … remember that ALL you have is His—
manage it well and excel in the gift of giving.*

Contents

ACKNOWLEDGMENTS

What a God we serve! To think He knew ahead of time that we would step into this new world of "authorship" to attempt to carry His message to His people regarding being faithful with His resources. We are grateful that He chose us and can only pray that these written words will serve to motivate many in the area of breaking down the barriers to generous giving.

We want to thank Tim Gunsolley from Cook Communications International; he had the courage to challenge us to consider this project and the confidence that this book would be worthwhile.

This book would not have been possible without our dear friend Bob Johnson. He gave hours and hours of help with writing and editing and communicating with everyone on the team.... We truly believe that the Lord placed you in our world "for such a time as this."

The book would be useless without a spiritual worldview, and we thank Greg Melendes for his deep insight and tireless work on the manuscript to make it truly "God's perspective."

And then there was the "A" team at David C. Cook. Thank you Dan Rich for spearheading the project and keeping us on point. Thank you Steve Parolini for your keen writer's eye and eternal perspective. Thanks also to Jaci Schneider and Ingrid Beck for never giving up and seeing us to the finish line.

Much gratitude to our family and friends who prayed continuously for this work. None of this would have been possible without your dedicated intercession.

In the end may glory be to God for His awesome ability to use two cracked pieces of clay to bring a story of stewardship to His people.

PREFACE

As the Christian movement faces the challenges of the twenty-first century, we find ourselves in a world of jolting contrasts between rich and poor and a turbulent global economy where there is little certainty or security. Yesterday's "haves" can become today's "have-nots" in the blink of an eye.

For those of us committed as followers of Jesus, the words of Philippians 4:12 (NASB) have poignant meaning in our time:

> *For I know how to live in humble means and I also know how to live in prosperity; in any and every circumstance I have discovered the secret of being filled and going hungry, both of having abundance and suffering need.*

This book is for those of us who are the privileged few, for those who have been blessed with abundance, however much that may be. It is our personal story about how God has repeatedly challenged us to go deeper in our responsibility as stewards of the resources He has seen fit to let us use. These pages describe our own journey of how we have determined, feeble as it is, to *"not lay up for ourselves treasures on earth, where moth and rust destroy, and where thieves break in and steal."*

Throughout our Christian experience, most of us have been taught that giving should be done out of obedience. The Bible says it. We should do it. Occasionally, we move beyond that to leveraging our resources for kingdom purposes in a way that taps into our passion and may even result in a profound sense of joy. But rarely do we move to a level of genuine sacrifice in how we wisely divest ourselves of our wealth. This book is a call to move to such a level.

These pages are also written from the perspective of a husband and wife who together are deeply immersed in the business world. We're not professional theologians or pastors. So what we describe here is from the level of the street, where we struggle daily not just to make a buck, but to practically and wisely put our hard-earned money to wise kingdom use.

At the very least, if these pages cause you to pause and reflect on what God wants done with your resources, then we will have succeeded. However, our prayer is that such reflection will turn into purposeful, sacrificial action that will release enormous, untapped resources as fuel for God's worldwide plans and purposes. Lord, make it so.

—Tony and Carin Amaradio

For we are God's workmanship, created in Christ Jesus to do good works, which God prepared in advance for us to do.

—*Ephesians 2:10*

CHAPTER ONE

Shaped for Life

⁓

Tony's Story

Dawn was breaking as Dad and I headed to Detroit's Eastern Market. It was a typical Michigan morning. The gray sky threatened rain as we made our Saturday pilgrimage. My dad was a blue-collar laborer who worked the night shift in a small factory and bought and sold tools on the side. But working two jobs still didn't provide enough to keep our family afloat. So each week we headed off to the market, where we would purchase as much produce as we could afford, then haul it back uptown and sell it to our neighborhood customers.

The stench of rotting vegetables and the frequent cry of sirens nearby kept us from lingering too long in the market, supplying an added element of urgency to our already hectic routine.

Once home I would load up my old, trusty red wagon and head with purpose into the neighborhood for the day. Unlike other kids, I wasn't earning extra spending money to buy toys and candy. Our household needed the income to help feed and meet the basic needs of a family of eight.

During these formative years God began to shape me into the person I would become. Natural gifts and talents began to emerge and personality traits were being forged. Even at a young age I was driven to succeed. Fighting off the natural fear of a six-year-old, I timidly approached house after house and offered my produce for sale. My first sale of the day gave me confidence for the next and the next until my wagon was empty. As I handed the profits to my dad, seeds of understanding about what it was like to truly make a contribution were sown in a very impressionable young heart.

This early success later spurred me to build my paper route into one of the largest in Detroit. The Rockwellian glamor of the paperboy, then a living piece of Americana, wore off quickly during those predawn winter mornings. It was a two-mile bicycle ride to the Detroit News distribution station, then back to my neighborhood where I faithfully delivered the news, weather, and sports to a still-sleeping audience.

Pinched between Lake Erie and Lake Huron, Detroit is doomed to endure long, cold, damp winters—and I was one of the chosen few to greet the coldest moments of each day. My clothing was no match for the harsh weather, and I recall returning home on many mornings with hands and feet nearly frostbitten. In spite of the bitter cold, an enormous German shepherd, and the constant pangs of loneliness—no small occupational hazards to a ten-year-old—my route grew from 11 customers to nearly 150. Little did I know that my entrepreneurial gift of building businesses would play such a big role in my life.

As I entered high school my motivation shifted and I was driven to excel in sports and academics. Earning all-state honors in basketball and graduating near the top of my class, my next stop was the University of Michigan, where I played Big Ten basketball for the Wolverines. Though I loved basketball, the reality eventually set in that there was only so much room in the NBA for six-foot guards! Sadly, realizing I was not going pro, I turned my focus entirely on my education and graduated from U of M with a BBA in 1974. Three years later I earned my MBA in finance from the University of Detroit.

Though I did not realize it, God was continuing to shape me during my college years. Yet, like so many "self-made men," in my own prideful mind I believed I had accomplished all this on my own. I was never at a loss for self-initiative or self-confidence.

At a very early age I decided I did not want to live in the same economic circumstances that marked my childhood, so my determination to be successful drove my every move. Even my decision to become a Christian at a Catholic Bible study did little to change how I went about pursuing my desire to become financially successful. I believed that if I was going to succeed, then my destiny was in my own hands. My measuring stick was marked by dollar signs, and I was determined to be a millionaire by the age of thirty!

Graduation day came in 1977, and I was ready to make my mark on the world. Ford Motor Company recruited me to enter their "fast track" management development program. I was poised for a future of prosperity and security—leaving the life of "just making ends meet" in my rearview mirror.

Before I was to report to Ford I had one more interview—with a well-known financial services company. In that interview I was introduced to the concept of an unlimited income. The absence of a salary cap, however, was not absent of risk. Could I survive and thrive on a commission-driven income? In the end, the potential to earn an income much greater than that of Ford was too big a lure for my youthful and expanding ego. I turned down the Ford Motor Company offer and launched my career in the financial services industry.

My first million-dollar year came in 1980, one year earlier than my target of thirty years old. Then a new thought germinated: Since earning a million was so easy, why not become a billionaire? I had it all—a big house, fancy cars, plush vacations, and money to spare—the Prodigal Son would have been jealous. Why not? I'd earned it, didn't I? Though I was attending church and men's Bible studies, I was so obsessed with wealth that I didn't let God interfere as I set and met my goals.

I was out of control.

That's when God decided to intervene.

My self-centered way of life had taken over and the Lord stepped back and let me have MY way. In the search for my next million I neglected my wife and daughters, eventually leading to a bitter divorce and substantial financial loss. He also allowed a series of business setbacks that left me broken, desolate, and wallowing in self-pity. I was lost, and I had nobody to blame but myself.

Yet even in this condition, when least deserving, God is a God of second chances and I was given my second chance when I married my business partner Carin on November 1, 1986. Having to start over financially due to one of the "consequences" of divorce, I was determined to do things differently. With a shared faith in Jesus as our Lord and Savior, with our Christ-centered commitment to our second marriages, we continued on the journey of life.

An unexpected event interrupted our newfound tranquility. Carin's mom, suffering from breast cancer, had passed away earlier that year. Taking advantage of Carin's involvement with her mother during this time, a trusted employee embezzled a healthy six-figure sum from our company. Carin eventually traced the source to a faulty key on an office typewriter—leading to the confession and termination of the embezzler.

The tests and trials continued. Soon thereafter I found myself facing my former employer in a very public legal battle, one I believed I would win. We continued to face one crisis after another, with this pattern dragging on for years. I found myself publicly humiliated and financially ruined, again. I was steeped in personal anguish and at the end of my rope. In the middle of the night of September 11, 1996, I lay prostrate on the floor, weeping, crying out to God. I was ready to give up everything—the business and our entire lifestyle. Though in college I had made the decision to trust Him for the forgiveness of my sins, I didn't understand what it meant to trust Him with my life—to allow Him to be my Lord! But on that night it was a full and true surrender, a time of flowing forgiveness and grace. In those hours Jesus Christ assumed His rightful position as not only my Savior but also my Lord.

I now refer to that night as my "carpet burn story" because of the hours I spent on my knees. From that night forward, I have held tight to Scripture verses that state without equivocation one of the most important things I discovered: that all I am and all I have belongs to God and God alone.

> Do not worship any other god, for the LORD, whose name is Jealous, is a jealous God.
> —Exodus 34:14

> For the LORD your God is a consuming fire, a jealous God.
> —Deuteronomy 4:24

God miraculously resolved the pending legal battle. I was free to continue practicing in the financial services industry, but far more wonderful, I was free to serve my Lord in a new and deeper way.

Today, as president of Select Portfolio Management, Inc., I share the leadership of our firm with my wife, Carin. Together we serve thousands of clients all over the United States. My major role is to operate as the chief strategist, advising our clients in the area of integrated wealth management. God has blessed me far beyond what I deserve. He not only restored the business but He also has prospered it beyond all of my early presumptive expectations. And He has done all this for His own glory, not mine!

Now my goals and motivation are far different. My earthly balance sheet will never reach one billion dollars. Instead, my focus now is on building our eternal balance sheet that will perpetuate through all eternity. What made the difference? I came to the realization that everything I own really belongs to Him. To some, that may sound like a foolish notion. To others, it might seem like a simple idea. It was neither. But it *was* the smartest business decision I have ever made.

Carin's Story

Less than a half mile away in East Detroit, not far from where Tony and his dad made their weekly produce run, another life was being shaped. I grew up in a middle-class family and lived a very normal and uneventful life—yet like Tony, I was being prepared for a future I could never imagine.

The first of two daughters, I relished my position as the center of my parents' universe until I was five years old. I was shaken from this lofty status with the birth of my sister, Cheryl, definitely an intrusion into my young and self-focused world. We grew up as typical sisters. Like many older siblings, I heaped good-natured "abuse" on her, and yet she still looked up to me. Today we remain extremely close even though we live on opposite sides of the country.

My dad and my uncle were partners and part owners of Thompson-Cain Meat Company, a wholesale distributor whose primary customers were hotels, restaurants, and schools.

Mom didn't work a traditional job during my childhood years, but she was very involved in local volunteer work. She dedicated much of her efforts to the Girl Scouts and eventually served as president of our local council. We were a devout Lutheran family, and as such, Mom made weekly church attendance mandatory. Her family was always her priority, and she was the glue that kept us together. She hosted an annual Christmas party in our home that included numerous extended family members—a gathering that tested the capacity of the phrase "full house." Her impact on my life continues to touch our family today.

My growing up years were typical of a young, carefree girl. Within the bounds of a traditional middle-class family I felt safe, secure, and loved. I never hesitated to join in any competition, enjoying nothing more than outrunning the boys in elementary school. In high school I competed in track and field in the sprints and hurdles, and I discovered a strong competitive streak that survives to this day.

I learned the virtue of hard work at a young age by babysitting and working at a beach snack shop. At sixteen I began to work the old-fashioned switchboard at my dad's company, and later moved into the invoice and billing department. From the very beginning I wanted to make sure no one could say I was simply skating by because my dad was the boss. I was determined to be an excellent employee so I tried to work harder than anyone else. I recall going out for early morning runs, showering, and then drying my hair by hanging my head out the car window—and still making it to work by 5:30 a.m. Perhaps being the oldest sibling breeds a self-imposed burden of responsibility. Whatever the reason, I determined I was not going to disappoint myself, my uncle, or especially my dad.

Neither of my parents attended college so it was important to them to provide an advanced education for their children. It was always assumed that I would go to college. While rummaging through some memorabilia recently I found a fill-in-the-blank book titled *This Is Me*. There, in the stiff penmanship of a ten-year-old, I boldly wrote, "Someday I will attend Michigan State University." Upon graduation from high school I applied only to MSU and was accepted. Another question in that book was "If I had a thousand dollars I would …," and I had written: "Send half of it to missions and spend half on useful things." Another question was, "If I had ONLY ONE wish I would wish that …" and I had written: "Everyone would know about Jesus." So the Lord was already forming my ministry—giving with a specific passion for evangelism.

Leaving home was not a traumatic experience for me since it was only ninety miles from Detroit to Lansing, the home of the MSU Spartans. Beyond my parents' expectations, my decision to go to college was an easy one. Many of my friends were going on to school. It was the thing to do. Having no clear goal in mind, the first two years of business college passed by swiftly. Entering my third year of studies, I had to decide on a major. Still lacking focus, I simply opened the college catalog and without planning or forethought selected retailing of clothing and textiles as my major. What I failed to consider at the time was the typical retail career entailed long hours—and relatively low pay.

Soon after college I married a young man I had known since I was thirteen. My marriage seemed normal and uneventful, not unlike my childhood. Yet it soon became obvious that our relationship was not based on a strong commitment to one another. We drifted into mutual coexistence, two people under one roof who were growing and going in different directions.

During this time I was a manager of a high-end women's retail store in a fashionable Detroit mall. On one of those rare occasions when I took the day off, a young, polished man walked into the store. He inquired if there might be a good saleswoman who would be interested in a high-paying sales position. The manager on duty admitted the salespeople in the store were not the quality he was seeking, but there was a young manager who was very good and well-liked by everyone. "But she doesn't happen to be working today," she said. The mystery shopper left, but not before leaving his business card with the manager. "Tell her to give me a call," he said, as he turned and walked out.

When I returned to work the next day she handed me his card. I looked at it, but quickly determined there was no way I would call this guy! He called again. And again. He was persistent! Finally, my curiosity overcame my good sense and I committed to an interview. On July 3, 1979, I met Tony Amaradio for the first time.

Though we tried to hide it, our relationship was sparked by instant mutual attraction. Even in the early days of our business partnership I did not want others to think I was receiving preferential treatment from Tony so I reverted to the "overdrive" mode I'd perfected during my days in the meat plant. No one was going to outperform me. I remember one New Year's Eve when everyone else was partying, I was alone at the office, working out the old year and working in the new.

In spite of our attempts to put protective barriers between us, Tony and I fell in love. Though our marriages were irreparably broken the ensuing battles that raged in our minds and hearts left us wallowing in a pool of guilt and shame. After struggling over the biblical legitimacy of our relationship that had spanned over seven years, we came to understand God's grace and forgiveness in the matter of our divorces. He offered us a chance to start over and on November 1, 1986, we decided to marry and to dedicate ourselves to building a godly marriage and a God-honoring business.

Soon after our wedding day we received two unexpected and very unwanted "gifts." The first was the news that one of our employees had embezzled close to $200,000 from our company. As his scheme began to unravel the embezzler tried to divert our focus by concocting a class-action lawsuit against Tony. He was eventually exposed and terminated, but our troubles were far from over … and would not be for another ten years!

In 1990, Tony moved to another company, sending his previous employer into attack mode. Tony was the company's highest producing broker, and the company feared other brokers—and clients—would follow him out the door. This led to a public battle that played itself out in local newspapers. Just when we had turned some corners in our personal lives, our business blew up in our faces!

We were confused and hurt. It didn't make sense. Of course our first thoughts were filled with self-condemnation. Were these the consequences of our failures in our former lives? Was this God's way of getting our attention? Every day was filled with new anxieties. We were battling a big organization with deep pockets. The embezzling employee solicited clients to file complaints against Tony that were used to lodge a formal complaint with the National Association of Securities Dealers (NASD). Even the slightest ray of hope would have carried us from day to day. Instead we were engulfed by despair.

It was in this darkest hour that Tony cried out to God in the night. He finally surrendered. He dropped his gloves and stopped fighting a fight he could not win. He was beaten and broken, but above all he was ready to do whatever God wanted him to do.

The phone rang early the next morning. It was the attorney working on our case. Before the attorney said a word, Tony told him he was ready to get out of the business. Totally ignoring Tony's remark, the attorney said, "Tony, you may want to sit down. Our opposition wants to settle!" At first I was skeptical. After all, we were so far apart that we couldn't have hoped for a reasonable settlement. But it became very clear God was working behind the scenes, and we could feel the burden lifting. Rather than risk a long and expensive fight in federal court, and the greater risk of losing, our opposition agreed to a very reasonable settlement. In hindsight, it may have been better to continue the fight to fully exonerate Tony, but at this point we were physically, emotionally, and financially drained.

Life finally seemed to move to normalcy. God continued to bless us in the days that followed, and today my role at Select Portfolio Management, Inc. is that of chief compliance officer, focusing on the operational side of the business.

Only the Beginning

We wanted to introduce ourselves by being transparent with you, not hiding or glossing over the past sins and struggles in our lives. We know from reading the Bible that God is in the restoration business, and we are so grateful that He loved us enough to forgive and restore us. Our lives are still under construction, and though we still fall short, like the apostle Paul we press on toward the goal. We place our trust in the only sure thing in life, our Lord and Master, Jesus Christ.

Today we stand in awe of God's grace. We recognize how, from childhood, God began to shape each of our lives. We see how He has transformed us through the hardest days. He continues to bless us far more than we can ever imagine. And He has done all this for a purpose—so that He might use our gifts and talents to do the work He prepared in advance for us to do.

THE EARTH IS THE LORD'S, AND EVERYTHING IN IT, THE
WORLD, AND ALL WHO LIVE IN IT; FOR HE FOUNDED IT
UPON THE SEAS AND ESTABLISHED IT UPON THE WATERS.

—Psalm 24:1–2

CHAPTER TWO

Starting Over

⁓

Describing Troy Phelan as an unhappy billionaire would be an understatement.

"I once owned all the appropriate toys," he said, "the yachts and jets and blondes, the homes in Europe, the farms in Argentina, an island in the Pacific, thoroughbreds, even a hockey team. But I've grown too old for toys."

Growing more ill and more disillusioned each day, Phelan began to see money in a different light. His quest for more of it had driven his every activity. He now realized his money and his life were tragically misspent.

"The money is the root of my misery," Phelan said, moments before he radically rewrote his will. He redirected virtually all his assets from his three ex-wives and six children to a missionary serving in the jungles of Brazil. That missionary was a daughter whose existence he had concealed from family and friends since her birth.

Before the ink could dry on the new will, Phelan jumped to his death from the fourteenth floor of his corporate headquarters.

Fiction? Yes, written by the gifted John Grisham in his book *The Testament*. Truth? Yes. Though few people choose to take their own lives in such dramatic fashion, many people like Phelan have pursued money and possessions in the hope of finding meaning and fulfillment in life. While far from suicidal, we too had been heading down that same path of unchecked accumulation. One day we would have awakened to realize exactly what Phelan did— that money does not bring ultimate satisfaction. Yet before it was too late, and only by God's grace, we were given the opportunity to reassess and develop a new set of values regarding the material things of this world.

The Turning Point

It's not like we weren't giving. At the time we were diligent about giving 10 percent of our income to the Lord, which amounted to a fair sum of money from most people's point of view.

Then we were invited to a conference on the topic of giving. Having participated at similar events in the past we weren't all that excited about attending, even though a highly respected and close friend of ours had personally extended the invitation. For me, Tony, it was a question of priorities. Did we really have the time to carve out of our busy schedules in order to attend another event? Would what we learned be worth the time we invest to attend?

Carin didn't want to go either, but for entirely different reasons.

Carin considers herself a quiet and somewhat private person. Putting her name on that list of attendees would be counter to who she was and to what she understood about giving. She doesn't like to talk to others about what she gives, nor did she want to hear others talking about what they give.

In spite of our misgivings we attended the conference. It featured a number of well-known Christian speakers, but also included testimonies from businesspeople, who like us, had invested much in God's kingdom. God used the testimony of one such man to transform our lives. Although I cannot remember his exact words, I will never forget the heart of his message.

He told us to imagine entering our conference room, closing the door, and placing all of our earthly possessions on the conference table. He challenged us to open that imaginary door, invite Christ to enter, and tell Him, "Lord and Savior, this is all Yours—do with it as You please!" His word picture hit home with a deep and lasting impact. Of course I had always affirmed that God owns everything, but at this moment, for the first time, my worldview regarding our possessions had finally intersected God's! I thought, "Nothing really belongs to us! Our portfolio, our business, our home ... even our children. Everything belongs to Him."

I immediately realized we needed to change how we managed His assets. There was one problem, however. What would Carin think? I didn't want to give her the idea I had gone off the deep end, driven by an emotional "high," so I strived to keep this new revelation quietly in my mind and heart. But over the next few days I continually found myself wrestling with God over this issue of ownership. Did I understand Him correctly? If so, how should I approach Carin with this?

Finally, we sat down and I rehearsed the speaker's comments, attempting to convey the deep impact they had on me. I told her I was convinced we needed to take a fresh look at what and how we give. Her response confirmed all God was doing in my own heart. "I'm ready," she said. "I've been convicted about our giving since the conference as well!" Our hearts were united as to what God wanted us to do, but we were still uncertain as to exactly *how* to do it.

Negotiations Begin

The next month I sat down to determine precisely what adjustments we would make to our giving habits. As I thought and prayed I found myself entering into negotiations with God.

Any good businessperson knows that the ability to negotiate is one of the most important skills of the game. Millions have been gained or lost by one wrong word, one moment of hesitation, one misread cue. We can even turn to the Bible for evidence of this truism. Remember when Abraham was negotiating for the survival of the cities of Sodom and Gomorrah, including the lives of his nephew Lot and his family? (See Genesis 18.) Abraham successfully moved God's number from fifty righteous people needed to save the cities downward to a mere ten. Of course, in the end God's purposes were fulfilled and the two cities ended up in cinders.

On this day my success was on par with that of Abraham. Numbers may have bounced around in our negotiation, but in the end, God's purposes would be fulfilled.

From the very beginning I felt I was bargaining from a position of strength. Research shows that only 3 to 5 percent of Christians meet the biblical charge of giving 10 percent, and yet we were consistently meeting or exceeding that amount. Certainly God was aware of that fact. Yet I admitted we needed to give more and offered 20 percent. I waited, but no trumpets sounded from heaven.

I upped the ante to 30 percent. Still, no affirmation from God. Okay, 40 … 50 … 60 percent? Nothing. Finally, thinking I finally understood His silence, I caved. "I get it now. Instead of giving You 10 percent and keeping 90 percent for ourselves, You want us to give You 90 percent and keep the other 10 percent for ourselves!"

"Tony," I sensed God saying, "you still don't get it. It's not a matter of how much of your money you give Me; it's a matter of recognizing who owns it."

God reminded me of the testimony of the man at the conference to bring me to my senses. I thought I had learned this lesson at the conference, but how quickly I reverted to my old mind-set. Thankfully, God is a patient teacher. When He presented the truth to me again, *this* time I got it.

Negotiations ended. It was time to seek Him for the first step of this new journey.

A New Starting Point: God Owns It All

God initiated the process of our radical worldview change regarding possessions by renewing our minds in three critical areas of life.

The first was articulated by David, a man whose own life began in the rocky sheep pastures of Israel and ended on its throne.

> *The earth is the LORD's, and everything in it, the world, and all who live*
> *in it; for he founded it upon the seas and established it upon the waters.*
> *—Psalm 24:1–2*

We had always believed this, even though we didn't live like we believed it. Yet our understanding of this truth has only deepened in the years since God began to reorder our financial paradigm. We came to realize David's declaration of God's proprietorship over the earth, and everything upon it, was tied to His very creation of it.

> *Now the earth was formless and empty, darkness was over the surface*
> *of the deep, and the Spirit of God was hovering over the waters.*
> *—Genesis 1:2*

There is an English legal proverb that asserts, "Possession is nine-tenths of the law." Well, that's certainly impressive, but God trumps that with the fact that creatorship is *100 percent* of the law! God owns everything because He *created* everything. In light of this reality, who were we to attach the words *my* or *our* to anything on this earth? God made it clear to us that He wants us not only to accept His grace, He wants us to acknowledge His ownership of our lives and our possessions.

To be honest, while Carin and I have come to recognize that the assets in our possession do not belong to us, living out that reality has not been without its struggles. We live in a very nice home, and we drive nice cars. We don't want to rationalize our purchasing decisions with the comforting argument that we could be living in a larger home or driving more luxurious cars, as though our "downsizing" has gained us favor with God. That sounds no better than the Pharisees' claims. Rather, we strive to allow God to lead us in our purchases. As we follow His leading we know we own what He wants us to own, and we can enjoy what He has given us to enjoy. Being human we are always faced with the temptation to covet, but God faithfully reminds us that all we have is His and that He has given it to us for a purpose higher than our personal pleasure (Hag. 2:6–9).

But there is a deeper struggle, one that goes back to my days of selling vegetables from a wagon and delivering newspapers in bitter Detroit winters. Having experienced poverty, I have found it difficult to escape the gnawing reality of it regardless of how much we have accumulated. And with the uncertainty of the financial world, there is always the temptation to allow a paralyzing fear of poverty to take control. Could it happen again? Is there a chance we will run out of money? It is at these times the Lord calms my heart with His words of comfort in Luke:

> *"Therefore I tell you, do not worry about your life, what you will eat; or about your body, what you will wear. Life is more than food, and the body more than clothes. Consider the ravens: They do not*

sow or reap, they have no storeroom or barn; yet God feeds them.
And how much more valuable you are than birds! Who of you by
worrying can add a single hour to his life? Since you cannot do this
very little thing, why do you worry about the rest?"
                                                —Luke 12:22–26

Yes, we *could* lose it all—yet God promised He would always
meet our needs. Even if it was all taken away, we would still have
Christ, "in whom are hidden all the treasures of wisdom and knowledge" (Col. 2:3).

A New Role: We Are Only Stewards

Acknowledging God as the owner of everything relegates us to mere
caretakers or custodians—in biblical terms, servants or stewards of
His possessions.

None of these terms conjures up the calling in life we envi-
sioned when we first established our educational goals, career
paths, or investment portfolios. I never anticipated doing what
somebody else wanted me to do—I expected to reach the status
of life where people would do *my* bidding. After all, what is the
purpose of money if it doesn't allow you to do what you want?

Yet a correct view of God's world transforms the role of servant
into a high calling—especially if one serves the Master well. Jesus
put it into story form like this:

"Again, it [the kingdom of heaven] will be like a man going on a journey, who called his servants and entrusted his property to them. To one he gave five talents of money, to another two talents, and to another one talent, each according to his ability. Then he went on his journey. The man who had received the five talents went at once and put his money to work and gained five more. So also, the one with the two talents gained two more. But the man who had received the one talent went off, dug a hole in the ground and hid his master's money.

"After a long time the master of those servants returned and settled accounts with them. The man who had received the five talents brought the other five. 'Master,' he said, 'you entrusted me with five talents. See, I have gained five more.'

"His master replied, 'Well done, good and faithful servant! You have been faithful with a few things; I will put you in charge of many things. Come and share your master's happiness!'

"The man with the two talents also came. 'Master,' he said, 'you entrusted me with two talents; see, I have gained two more.'

"His master replied, 'Well done, good and faithful servant! You have been faithful with a few things; I will put you in charge of many things. Come and share your master's happiness!'

"Then the man who had received the one talent came. 'Master,' he

said, 'I knew that you are a hard man, harvesting where you have
not sown and gathering where you have not scattered seed. So I was
afraid and went out and hid your talent in the ground. See, here is
what belongs to you.'

"His master replied, 'You wicked, lazy servant! So you knew that I
harvest where I have not sown and gather where I have not scattered
seed? Well then, you should have put my money on deposit with the
bankers, so that when I returned I would have received it back with
interest."

"'Take the talent from him and give it to the one who has the
ten talents. For everyone who has will be given more, and he
will have an abundance. Whoever does not have, even what he
has will be taken from him. And throw that worthless servant
outside, into the darkness, where there will be weeping and
gnashing of teeth.'"

—Matthew 25:14–30

Jesus told this story, utilizing symbols and practices that were
culturally relevant, to illustrate important spiritual truths regarding God's kingdom and His rule over both earth and eternity.
Through this parable of a financially privileged man and his three
servants, He teaches principles about the master's expectations and
the servants' reward that apply to us today—and that will affect us
into eternity.

The Trust Factor

As the man entrusted his possessions to the servants, so God has entrusted us with His possessions. This in itself is an awesome privilege and responsibility. Think of it ... God chose us to steward, first and foremost, the gospel, as well as the resources to spread it among those who need to hear it. Already this role of steward has taken on a whole new weight of significance. If I am going to be a servant, I want to serve *this* Master!

Let's take a closer look at this parable and what it means for us today.

A SETTLEMENT OF ACCOUNTS

Upon the return of the master, each servant appeared privately before him. In 2 Corinthians 5:10 and 1 Corinthians 3:12–15, the apostle Paul also mentions the reality of each Christian's private audience before the throne of Christ. At that appointed time each of us will give an account for what we have done in this lifetime. Notice that each of the first two servants came before their master not in fear but in confidence. They knew their master well, knew what it would take to please him, and they knew that they performed accordingly. Knowing and doing God's will gives us confidence to stand before Him with a clear conscience, whether here and now on earth or later before His throne.

AN ASSESSMENT

The servants who were given five and two talents were highly praised and called "faithful" by the master. They were so judged, first, because they diligently cared for and multiplied what belonged to another—in this case their master's funds. Second, they treated the "few things" of the master as though they were of great value. They defined faithfulness in this context and thus left us all with an example to follow as we seek to look after the things that God has entrusted to us (Deut. 8:18, Eccl. 5:19).

As a side note, while a talent was a considerable amount of money in Jesus' time, the master still refers to five and two of them as if they were pocket change—little things. This puts our present-day portfolios, regardless of their size, in proper perspective. No matter how we look at it, it's just a very, very small part of all that belongs to God. In truth, there is no shortage of resources to accomplish His work on earth. They only need to be allocated for His purposes and for His glory.

A REWARD

The master rewarded the two faithful servants, not with a fat Christmas bonus check, but with a compliment and with more work. Today that might elicit a sarcastic "Gee, thanks" when the boss leaves the room—but not so in God's economy.

Saints throughout the history of the church have lived in poverty, suffered illness and hardship, left family and home, sacrificed earthly goods and life, all in order to hear the words "Well done" in the presence of their Lord. God does not ask this level of service from all of us—but He does require us to labor in His fields in various capacities. We know that God has shaped us, through the faithful stewardship of His resources, to facilitate the preaching of the gospel both at home and abroad. We do this with all our hearts in hopes that someday we too will hear "Well done" from Him.

Beyond His affirmation, the two faithful servants were given responsibility over "many things." Having been tested and proven, the master allowed them to expand their service into wider areas of their expertise. In the same way, faithful service to our Lord is rewarded by greater opportunities to serve Him here and now.

Finally, the master invites them to share in their "master's happiness." Many Bible scholars feel this was an invitation to join him at his table for a feast. Of course this was a high honor for anyone, especially for servants. Beyond honor, however, it provided a rare time of intimacy with the master. We have found that money cannot bring ultimate satisfaction. Only living under the intimate shelter of the Lord's approval can.

An Encouragement and a Warning

It's interesting to note the difference between the response of the third servant and the first two. He opens his defense by calling his master a "hard" or stern man. He believed that his master was someone who gained maximum profit while expending minimum energy in the sowing and harvesting processes. In other words, he knew his master was an excellent investor. Yet it's obvious he did not know the master the way the other two did. If he did, and if his heart was to please his master, he surely would have responded differently.

Because he did the very least with what was put into his hands, the master took back his one and only talent. God has given each of us talents (in the modern sense of the word) and resources. If we use them as He wishes He will develop and multiply them, ultimately bringing greater glory to Himself. If, however, we fail to use them as He wishes they bring no gain to us or to His kingdom. This parable should serve as an encouragement and a warning to those of us to whom much has been entrusted.

Before moving on we want to make one thing clear—giving our time, talent, or treasure does not get us to heaven. Eternal life is a free gift, secured by our faith in the death, burial, and resurrection of Christ. It can't be bought or bartered. Our desire to be the best stewards possible comes from grateful and obedient hearts. We don't give to gain eternal life. We give as an act of worship.

We also want to caution against wrong teaching that encourages giving in order to get more in return. The "prosperity gospel" has been spread liberally around the world, and in truth it is no gospel (good news) at all. The "give so you will gain" mind-set has confused and misled many believers, taking their eyes from the cross of the eternal Christ and turning them instead toward that which rusts and rots.

A New Mind-set: How, Not How Much

As we began to understand and accept these truths—that God owns everything and that our role is that of stewards—we were faced with a significant, lingering question: "So, how much should we give?" And on the flip side of that question we discovered another unanswered question: "So, how much is enough to live on?" Answering either question would provide the answer to the other. Unfortunately, we have found that there is no quick and easy formula.

But here's what we did begin to see. God wasn't impressing on us a number, but the posture of our hearts. He was moving us along a path from reluctant givers to obedient givers, and we still had a long way to go before reaching His ultimate goal. When we were tempted to think that we might be giving too much, the words of Jesus in the temple reminded us that such an amount does not exist:

> As he looked up, Jesus saw the rich putting their gifts into the temple treasury. He also saw a poor widow put in two very small copper coins. "I tell you the truth," he said, "this poor widow has put in more than all the others. All these people gave their gifts out of their wealth; but she out of her poverty put in all she had to live on."
>
> —Luke 21:1–4

Back when we gave a self-satisfying 10 percent of our income, we were no better than the rich people Jesus witnessed in the temple. We had a quiet, yet self-righteous air, believing we were doing all we should—and, notably, more than most. Though a large amount to many, in reality, our offering was a very small part of our total resources. Like the rich people in the temple, we gave out of our wealth. It never hurt.

Two very small copper coins doesn't seem like much, does it?

Our smallest coin—the penny—may have a different value today, but the image we get from imagining someone putting two pennies in an offering probably isn't so far removed from what Jesus was relating. But here's the key: She didn't just give the two coins that happened to be in her purse at the time. Not just spare change rattling around in a pocket. She "put in all she had to live on" into the treasury. Hers was not only the ultimate act of giving—but it was also an extraordinary act of faith. We don't know if it was a struggle for her to pull out those last two coins. Luke doesn't say. But when she dropped them in the treasury she completely threw herself upon the graciousness of the One and Only Person whom she trusted to ultimately supply all her needs.

Could we give like that? Should we give like that? As we looked to Scripture we found much written about the subject of giving—from Israel's tithe (first mentioned in Lev. 27:30), to the rich young man (Luke 18:18–29), to Ananias and Sapphira (Acts 5:1–10), and on through to Paul's instructions to the Corinthian church (1 Cor. 16:1–2 and 2 Cor. 8—9). Perhaps our struggle to know what to give would have been easier had God settled on a number or percentage for all incomes and life situations. But there is no such indicator given in the New Testament.

And so, along with a new starting point and a new role in His kingdom, God had to give us a new mind-set regarding giving. He continues to show us that *how* we give is more important than how much we give. It is an ongoing process, and we continue to learn. We certainly do not want to give the impression that this has been easy or that we have figured out a system that makes giving "comfortable." Giving as God wants us to give involves battles in our own hearts. Like the story of the woman in the temple, it's obvious that God desires us to do more than simply give out of our wealth. He wants us to trust *Him*, not our resources, to supply all our needs.

FOR WHERE YOUR TREASURE IS, THERE
YOUR HEART WILL BE ALSO.

—*Matthew 6:21*

CHAPTER THREE

Barriers to Giving

~

Americans proclaim themselves the most generous nation on earth.

False.

And true.

According to recent studies by the Organization for Economic Cooperation and Development (OECD), the United States Government ranks as low as twenty-second in international giving based on donations in relation to Gross National Product.

Yet, the country's largest charity evaluator, Charity Navigator, states American *citizens* gave $306 BILLION dollars, or 2.2 percent of GNP, to charities in calendar year 2007. To put it in context, in 2007, Americans gave roughly $40 billion less than Exxon earned in total revenue the previous year, and $100 billion more than General Motors' 2006 revenues. Of that $306 billion, one out of every three dollars was given to religious centers. No doubt a bull market and favorable tax laws have fostered a giving climate, but no matter how you look at it, Americans are an incredibly generous people.

According to the Association for Fundraising Professionals, evangelical Christians are among the most likely sectors of the population to donate. Collectively we may have much to be proud of ... but when it's my turn, or your turn, to stand before our Lord, flag waving and rosy statistics will be of little value to us.

Like the servants in the parable of the talents, on that day each of us will stand before God and "receive what is due him for the things done while in the body, whether good or bad" (2 Cor. 5:10). We know that our sins were paid for by Christ, so these will not be the focus of this assessment. Instead it will be the ultimate payday—the parable of the three stewards come to life. For fulfilling the good works prepared for us (Eph. 2:8–10) we will receive a reward that will never perish (1 Cor. 3:12–15). However, for those tasks left undone, or for those tasks done in the name of God yet in the power of our own flesh, *there can be no reward.* Our salvation will not be at risk, but our "rewards" will.

This truth of ultimate reward and loss drove Carin and me to the Word in order to further understand God's thoughts on the topic of giving. Though we didn't realize it at the time, we were actually developing a theology of giving. (We'll cover this more in the next chapter.) We also examined our lives to determine the barriers that had prevented us from giving in a way that corresponded with what we were learning. We discovered the same barriers faced by many Americans, Christian or not, but we could not "hide behind the big guy" in the class picture. God was speaking to us directly. We knew the barriers had to come down, and though it would not be easy, we had to trust that He would give us grace to form a new worldview toward our possessions and how we handled them.

The Tax Barrier

No friends of Jesus, the Pharisees approached Him in hopes of trapping Him in a catch-22 situation that would land Him before the governor. Couching their question in lofty praise, they asked, "Is it right for us to pay taxes to Caesar or not?"

Seeing through their thinly veiled attempt at self-indictment, He answered:

> *"Show me a denarius [valued at about a day's pay] Whose portrait and inscription are on it?"*

> *"Caesar's," they replied.*

> *He said to them, "Then give to Caesar what is Caesar's, and [give] to God what is God's."*
> —Luke 20:24–26

As His disciples we want to follow God's directive, so we faithfully pay the IRS all of what we owe—but giving any more than that amount would mean we're dipping into God's treasury! This is true of our personal finances, and we provide the same advice to our clients.

In recent years, tax laws have fostered giving and also rewarded those who have generously done so. But this is true only to a point. In most cases, tax deductions are allowed on donations up to roughly 50 percent of adjusted gross income. Donations above that are not deductible.

While the U.S. deduction cap is much more generous than those of other countries, a conflict often arises when God calls a person to give above that 50 percent level. Without a deduction the cost-benefit ratio of giving drops dramatically and deters some from taking that extra leap of faith—a leap that can challenge our obedience to God.

When we reached this impasse we knew God was moving us beyond our comfort zone. The admonition to "let go" may seem like a simple enough concept, but once we did let go, we found ourselves in unfamiliar territory with our giving no longer tied to deductions. Certainly we take advantage of deductions because they free even more resources to distribute where God wants them. But gaining a deduction was no longer a *prerequisite* to our giving. This freed our hearts much more than any deduction, and we found ourselves moving into a whole new realm of giving!

You may be thinking, "Are they serious? Why is this even an issue? Who in their right mind gives away more than half of what they earn?" We understand that for many, this level of giving may never be possible. We also believe that God is calling many others to give not just half of what they earn, but well beyond; people to whom He has given many resources to manage that can be used to greatly impact His kingdom. We advise these folks to "Let go." If

God is moving you into that zero-deduction zone of giving, boldly follow the call. Don't let the IRS rules stop you. After all, by now "Caesar" has already received his share!

The Principal Barrier

Giving from our surplus resources was easy. In fact, most people give out of their surplus, which is not a bad thing. But *radical* giving may mean tearing down another barrier—the one that protects your principal. That's right. God may be calling you to dip into principal that has been stashed away, earning interest year after year.

But doesn't this contradict the principles and practices of the entire financial services industry? Financial advisors typically encourage investors to put their principal in a lockbox and only use net profits to build greater assets. Principal remains untouchable even for the noblest of philanthropic purposes. It's the safe and wise thing to do.

However, it's only the safe and wise thing to do if it's what *God* wants you to do. But what if your earnings are not up to expectations and God has made it clear He wants you to give at a level that will force you to dig into principal? If God is calling you to fly in the face of this world's conventional wisdom—as He does in so many other areas of the Christian life—then we'd encourage you to reach for the key to your lockbox. Holding back may give some temporary sense of security. But that will evaporate. After all, what would be worse than to stand before Him, as the servant who buried his talent, and have nothing to show for the resources He put in our hands?

This question is more than hypothetical to us. One late December afternoon Carin and I sat down as we always do near year-end to analyze the income and expenses for the year. The news was good. Very good. It was an extraordinary year for our business and likewise for us. In my mind I had privately planned that I wanted to increase our giving by 20 percent that year if our income had increased accordingly. Well, the Lord loves to teach and stretch and often displays a real sense of humor. The numbers indicated a 71 percent increase for the year! My first reaction was disbelief and a prompt demand for a recount. How was this possible? After all, a seasoned business like ours might grow at a healthy 3–5 percent, but 71 percent? Once the numbers were confirmed a fleshly impulse drove me to attempt to implement MY plan of giving an additional 20 percent and sheltering the other 51 percent of the windfall. It seemed the reasonable thing to do. Thankfully, Carin rescued me from my folly. She confronted me with the question as to why I was placing limits on our giving and challenged me to consider giving the entire 71 percent. By loosening the grip on these unexpected profits we experienced the joy of giving even more to His kingdom work than we had anticipated. God continued to nudge us down the road … from reluctant, to obedient, and now, to joyful givers. Almost there? Not yet.

Certainly we all need to determine our life context and prepare ourselves for the seasons of life right around the corner. But we encourage Christ's followers, in the quietness of their own hearts, away from the din of advisors and family, to seek God's mind in this matter of giving at the peaks and through the valleys. We find that this helps us to evaluate our giving in light of our goals and reset them continually. It's during these precious times that God relieves the fears and temptations that arise from the day-to-day battle to grip or let go of what belongs to Him.

The Debt Barrier

Current American culture is steeped in the "inalienable right" to feel instant gratification. Forget that twenty-five years ago most of us didn't own a computer. Today we complain if we have to wait three nanoseconds to log on in the morning. In our pockets and purses we carry the equivalent of a telephone, camera, television, stereo, newspaper, message machine, typewriter, and telegraph— and panic if somebody "can't hear me now"!

If we are not in pursuit of faster, we are in pursuit of bigger. Bigger houses, bigger automobiles, bigger lifestyles. This quest for more makes it difficult for a family to outswim the tide of ensuing financial obligations and makes it easy to reach for the stack of credit cards.

Proverbs 22:7 states, "The rich rule over the poor, and the borrower is servant to the lender." If this is the case, then Americans are enslaved to creditors. Some statistical sources staked the average family consumer debt (not including a typical mortgage) at $8,200 in 2007. Consumer debt nearly quintupled from $355 billion in 1980 to $1.7 trillion in 2001, settling in at $2.5 trillion by 2007.

Living in an environment of entitlement and low-risk, high-yield investments leads to a false sense of self-worth that comfortably disguises greed in the trappings of need. It is tempting to overspend rather than delay or even forego gratification for God's higher purposes. Yet there are rewards for those who choose to seek, first and foremost, His kingdom.

Personal debt is not only an albatross, interest rates that border on usury deflect God's resources away from His intended purposes. Debt can ruin marriages, families, and the best of friends. That is why Paul admonished the believers in Rome to "Pay to all what is owed to them: taxes to whom taxes are owed, revenue to whom revenue is owed" (Rom. 13:7 ESV).

The Biggest Barrier of Them All

Like Nicodemus and the Samaritan woman before him, an affluent young man once approached Jesus to ask what he needed to do to obtain eternal life. When Jesus simply told him to follow the commandments given to Moses, he replied, "Teacher, all these I have observed from my youth."

This story would be significant if it were told in even one of the gospels, but it was recounted in detail by three writers, Matthew (19:16–22), Mark (10:17–22), and Luke (18:18–23). There is obviously a point that God, through these authors, wants to make.

The narratives are strikingly similar, yet only Mark precedes Jesus' answer with a look into His heart: "And Jesus, looking at him loved him, and said to him, 'You lack one thing: go, sell what you have, and give it to the poor, and you will have treasure in heaven;

and come, follow me'" (ESV). Sensing the sincerity of this young man, the heart of the Lord Jesus overflowed with love toward him. In spite of knowing the ultimate outcome of their discussion, He responded not in condemnation or condescension, but with the ultimate compassion. He told the man to cash in the only thing standing between him and eternal life—his earthly possessions—and join in fellowship with Lord of Lords.

If only … Jesus told the Samaritan woman at the well, "If you knew the gift of God and who it is that asks you for a drink, you would have asked him and he would have given you living water" (John 4:10). If only this young man had known what Jesus had offered him in exchange for things that rot and rust and mold, surely he would have gladly run off to do a "Bill and Melinda Gates" and be back at Jesus' side by the time the sun went down.

Instead we read, "disheartened by the saying, he went away sorrowful; for he had great possessions."

The young man, whose sincerity stirred the heart of Jesus, turned down the offer of an eternal relationship with God. You might want to read that sentence again. Do you see what he gave up? And why? He allowed his many possessions to prevent him from finding what he had earnestly been seeking since his youth. As it turned out, the biggest barrier of all was his heart, where he stored his treasure (Matt. 6:21).

Now I need to point out that the Scripture is *not* teaching that in order to have eternal life, people of means should sell all they have and give it all to the poor. This was not a global or universal command. If it was, why did Jesus let diminutive Zacchaeus off the hook with giving only half of his possessions in the next chapter of Luke (19:8–9)?

No, Jesus knew this man's heart. He wanted this man to divest himself of the idol that he cherished above the One True God. For him, it was his vast possessions. For another man it may be his attachment to Internet pornography. For a woman it may be the ongoing search for the fountain of youth. If we are honest with ourselves, most of us have more than one idol on our altars. And while our culture offers a pantheon of idols, by repeating this narrative three times God is making a point and then underlining it: To many of us, earthly possessions stand on a particularly high pedestal. Letting go of them is hard to do. Accepting that they are not ours, but His, is a tough truth to swallow. Being relegated to mere stewards is an even tougher one, especially for the type-A personalities who populate the highest financial stratosphere. So what is it that can cause us to loosen our grip on what we hold so near and dear?

> *And Jesus, looking at him loved him.*
> —*Mark 10:21* (ESV)

> *We love Him because He first loved us.*
> —*1 John 4:19* (NKJV)

For Christ's love compels us.
　　　　　　—2 Corinthians 5:14

We need to take our eyes off our possessions long enough to look into the loving heart of the Lord Jesus. And when we see His heart, we will be compelled to drop to our knees in acknowledgment of His ownership of *every* area of our lives. Our natural response will then be to live in response to His love and to give in response to His love.

Giving out of Love

It is no accident that, while God displayed His love in many ways, He did so most demonstratively through the act of giving.

For God so loved the world that he gave ...
　　　　　—John 3:16

This is how God showed his love among us: He sent his one and only Son.
　　　　　　—1 John 4:9

When we consider the topic of giving we need to keep in mind that while it involves obedience, it must be motivated first and

foremost by love. As we move into areas of wealth mission statements, giving strategies, and estate plans, it may be easy to transport
giving from the heart to the boardroom. Paul illustrated this danger
to the Corinthians by saying, "If I give all I possess to the poor and
surrender my body to the flames, but have not love, I gain nothing"
(1 Cor. 13:3). Whether your theological focus is the church or the
kingdom, keep in mind that *neither* one is a business. As we apply
the wisdom of the Word and the wisdom of the financial world,
we must always remember that giving is, and always should be, a
matter of the heart.

We must always remember that even if we gave away everything
it still does not remotely compare to the ultimate gift of love at
Calvary as Christ gave up His life to cover our sins and redeem us.

No one can serve two masters. Either he will hate the one and love the other, or he will be devoted to the one and despise the other. You cannot serve both God and Money.

—Matthew 6:24

CHAPTER FOUR

A Biblical Theology of Giving

—

When you think of Jesus' life and ministry it might seem incongruous that One with so little spoke so often about money. At times it was the main topic of His message, at others it was merely a prop used to help Him make a greater point.

The Old Testament is also replete with stories about men who God blessed with much, and men who lost it all. Through narrative, poetry, and proverb, He established principles of ownership, promises to bless, and warnings against greed and laziness. Overarching all these was the understanding that it was God who gave and God who withheld. Though not every reference to giving applies to us today (try putting a grain offering in the plate next Sunday!), all of the principles are as true and applicable as ever.

As we mentioned in the previous chapter, one of the first steps Carin and I took in this journey was to seek God's heart on the matter of giving as revealed in His Scriptures. In essence, we were forming a biblical theology of ownership and giving. Good theology is essentially knowing God intimately and knowing how He wants us to act upon that knowledge. We read many books about giving, attended seminars, and listened to sermons. Yet we needed to search and sift through His Word—like the Bereans seen in Acts—in order to more fully grasp the principles and commands in their various contexts.

As in all areas of doctrine, our first desire is to know Him, so we begin our search by looking at a few selected Scriptures that focus on God's manner of giving. Once we get an idea of what kind of giver God is, we will then look at some of the implications of these truths on us in our role as His stewards.

Withholding Nothing

HE GIVES OUT OF LOVE

The more we looked, the more it became clear that our God is a God who shows His love through giving. Of course this is not the only way He demonstrates His love to us. He predestined us to be His adopted sons out of love (Eph. 1:5). He chastens us out of love (Heb. 12:6). So many of His actions toward us are wrapped in love, and the ultimate was that of giving His Son to redeem us from a well-deserved fate:

> *For God so loved the world that he gave his one and only Son, that*
> *whoever believes in him shall not perish but have eternal life.*
> —*John 3:16*

This is how God showed his love among us: he sent his one and only Son into the world that we might live through him. This is love: not that we loved God, but that he loved us and sent his Son as an atoning sacrifice for our sins.

—1 John 4:9

John tells us in his first epistle that God *is* love, so everything He does is done out of His very nature. As we are all created in His image, it is not surprising to see people in every corner of the world—Christian and non-Christian alike—reflecting through generosity that very DNA God stamped upon us all. Of course those of us who are marked with the seal of the Holy Spirit understand and appreciate all the more the source of all generosity. It is this depth of love that caused John, the beloved apostle, to write, "We love [Him] because he first loved us" (1 John 4:19).

He Gives Sacrificially

On the basis of being the Creator, He is the owner of everything—but that does not mean that our God is not a sacrificial giver. Both the Father who sent and the Son who went experienced the pain of separation for the first time in eternity. Loved above all, Jesus was still forsaken by the Father as He carried the sins of the world on the cross. The anguish of His physical suffering was not to be compared to the spiritual suffering He experienced on our behalf.

This is how we know what love is: Jesus Christ laid down his life for us.
                              —1 John 3:16

I have been crucified with Christ and I no longer live, but Christ lives in me. The life I live in the body, I live by faith in the Son of God who loved me and gave himself for me.
                              —Galatians 2:20

Be imitators of God, therefore, as dearly loved children and live a life of love, just as Christ loved us and gave himself up for us as a fragrant offering and sacrifice to God.
                              —Ephesians 5:1–2

While He gives out of His abundance, He also gave His One and Only—and in doing so, demonstrated what sacrificial giving looks like.

HE GIVES FREELY

In spite of the pain of Their separation, God did not give the minimum, and He did not give reluctantly. The word *grace* means "undeserved favor." God did not stop at saving grace, He poured out grace in abundance for this life (2 Cor. 9:8). There should be no doubt in the life of the believer that he has, and always will have, all he needs to live a life that pleases our Lord.

For even the Son of Man did not come to be served, but to serve and to give his life as a ransom for many.

—*Mark 10:45*

He who did not spare his own Son, but gave him up for us all—how will he not also, along with him, graciously give us all things?

—*Romans 8:32*

For you know the grace of our Lord Jesus Christ, that though he was rich, yet for your sakes he became poor, so that you through his poverty might become rich.

—*2 Corinthians 8:9*

Many cultures in the world give solely with the expectation of receiving something of equal or greater value in return. Unfortunately, some in the Christian arena teach the same principle. This is the type of giving Jesus was challenging when He said, "I do not give to you as the world gives" (John 14:27).

God gives freely and abundantly. He will never be outgiven, and He will never be a debtor to anyone.

He Gives Constantly

From man's first tour of the garden of Eden (Gen. 1:28–31) to Christ's admonition not to worry about food or drink (Luke

12:27–31), it is apparent that God is constantly meeting the needs of His children.

First He promised the Counselor, the Holy Spirit (John 14:25–27), who would come and "teach you all things and will remind you of everything I have said to you." That promise was fulfilled in Acts chapter 2—and the Holy Spirit remains a guide to the universal church, the local church, and every individual believer.

He has also given gifts that keep on giving through His body, the church. In this way He has provided not only for the earthly needs of believers, He has provided for their spiritual needs as well. Before He ascended into heaven He "gave some to be apostles, some to be prophets, some to be evangelists, and some to be pastors and teachers, to prepare God's people for works of service" (Eph. 4:11–12).

He also gave each believer a spiritual gift, or gifts, "for the common good" (1 Cor. 12:7). It is not surprising that one of these is the gift of giving, as Paul writes in Romans 12:8: "[If a man's gift is] contributing to the needs of others, let him give generously," giving with the same heart with which God gives.

These four areas only crack open the door into the treasury of truth regarding our giving God. As we continue to study, we grow in our appreciation for what He has given to us so abundantly. And we rejoice because He has spiritually gifted us to "give generously." We have no reason to miss His calling in our lives, whether we have little or we have much.

How Should We Then Give?

Seeing God as the ultimate giver led us to continue our search of the Scriptures for truths regarding our responsibilities as His stewards—a search that continues to this day.

We've woven many scriptural truths throughout this book, but those that follow have deeply impressed us since the first days of our journey. They are not complex, but together they form the next layer of biblical truth used by God to change our worldview regarding kingdom investments.

WHAT GOD LOVES

From Genesis to Revelation it is obvious that, apart from His Son, man is the primary object of God's affection. Christ's love for the church is such that it is referred to as His bride. I believe it is significant, then, that in Proverbs 15:9, we learn He loves those who pursue righteousness. And look at what Paul writes:

> *Remember this: Whoever sows sparingly will also reap sparingly, and whoever sows generously will also reap generously. Each man should give what he has decided in his heart to give, not reluctantly or under compulsion, for God loves a cheerful giver. And God is able to make all grace abound to you, so that in all things at all times, having all that you need, you will abound in every good work. As it is written:*

> *"He has scattered abroad his gifts to the poor;*
> *his righteousness endures forever."*
> *   —2 Corinthians 9:6–9*

Something in the giving heart of God ignites when He sees His children give as He does. Parents can relate to this. Even a young boy brings joy to his parents when he attempts to imitate the way his father holds the oversized hammer—or a girl when she gets in the dirt and gardens alongside her mother. That joy increases as children grow older and they continue to follow in the footsteps of their parents. No longer is it mere imitation, nor is it out of compulsion. It is something they own. They have learned to love what their parents love, to the joy of the parents.

So it is when the cheerful giver gives. God, the eternal Father, sees His image reflected in His children. He knows they not only love Him, they have grown to love what He loves—and His joy is unsurpassed!

I think it's important to note that it's not always easy to be a cheerful giver. Giving when the economy is suffering, when the financial news is all "doom and gloom" can pose a great challenge to our ability to give joyfully. In over thirty years of practice as a wealth manager, I have never been more concerned about our economy. It's not natural to be joyful when things are tough all around. Thankfully, it is God Himself who grants us the ability to find joy in circumstances that otherwise might bring fear or worry. This is an ongoing challenge for all of us—to learn to trust God's provision and goodness and to celebrate our giving no matter what we're hearing on the nightly news.

Give When It Hurts

We have already recounted the story of the poor widow who placed her last two coins into the temple treasury. As Jesus stood by He surveyed her act of generosity and faith and assessed her gift of greater value than any other given that day. Obviously the temple treasurer would not agree with Him. Nor would the other donors.

Yet that assessment was true. Because she gave out of her poverty, because she gave all she had, her gift will weigh more through all eternity than all theirs combined.

Malcolm Forbes is attributed with saying, "He who dies with the most toys wins." His legacy in the world of business may be secure, but his measuring stick certainly isn't God's. Around the same time Forbes was building his empire, another young man gave his life in order to bring a remote and hostile people into the kingdom of God. Jim Elliot, in a letter to his wife Elisabeth, wrote, "He is no fool who gives up what he cannot keep in order to gain what he cannot lose." What different values derived from their opposing worldviews! Jim and four other missionaries—as the widow in the temple—gave all they had, and gained that which could not be lost (Mark 8:36).

How do you know you're giving when it hurts? Here's the short answer: If you are feeling stretched beyond your traditional comfort zone—for example, if you are hearing God ask you to dip into principal—then God is probably inviting you into sacrificial giving. And just as it is difficult through earthly efforts to be a cheerful

A NOTE TO THE RICH

How many times have you heard phrases like, "You can't take it with you," or "I never saw a hearse pulling a U-haul"? These quotes always draw nods and chuckles, but do they slow the race for the things of this world? Not so much. The Lord Jesus often warned the rich that their earthly possessions were of no value when it came to their eternal destiny. In his first letter to the young evangelist, Paul instructed Timothy not to simply remind the rich, or suggest to the rich, but twice told him to command the rich:

> Command those who are rich in this present world not to be arrogant nor to put their hope in wealth, which is so uncertain, but to put their hope in God, who richly provides us with everything for our enjoyment. Command them to do good, to be rich in good deeds, and to be generous and willing to share. In this way they will lay up treasure for themselves as a firm foundation for the coming age, so that they may take hold of the life that is truly life.
> —1 Timothy 6:17–19

It isn't class envy that drives Paul's words. It is his genuine concern for the rich. His intent is to have them focus their hope on God and to "take hold of the life that is truly life." God isn't trying to take anything away from us.... He's always trying to give us more! It's our choice. We can keep chuckling and pursuing a bigger portfolio, but we do so at the risk of disobeying God's clear command to be rich in good deeds.

giver, it is often difficult to give sacrificially without feeling some angst or struggling with obedience. This is just the reality of our constant battle with the flesh, with worldliness. It is by God's own gift of grace that we can find a way to give beyond what we might think is possible.

Giving out of abundance may feel good, but giving when it hurts brings Him greater glory.

A Silent Partner

God could not be any clearer about prideful motivation in giving than He is in this passage:

> "Be careful not to do your 'acts of righteousness' before men, to be seen by them. If you do, you will have no reward from your Father in heaven.

> "So when you give to the needy, do not announce it with trumpets, as the hypocrites do in the synagogues and on the streets, to be honored by men. I tell you the truth they have received their reward in full. But when you give to the needy, do not let your left hand know what your right hand is doing, so that your giving may be in secret. Then your Father, who sees what is done in secret, will reward you."
>
> —Matthew 6:1–4

Pride is a powerful and devious motivator. Though we may initially give out of true humility, sometimes we feel the tug of temptation to let that giving go to our heads. In fact, the writing of this very book could point us in the dangerous direction of pride. So what are we to do? Should we stay silent and not speak at all about giving? No, God has called us to share what we have learned. And that's the fine line we walk—we don't have any interest in telling you what we give, but we surely do want to share the joy and wonder of what we have learned about how we are to give.

But there is another reason to fight against pride and God has deeply impressed upon us this truth. Reward and loss are the two results of investing in the marketplace, and the consequences are no different in God's economy. We don't keep our giving private to avoid the barrage of requests—sooner or later, if you are a giver, you will be found! Rather, our desire to remain silent partners is to receive and retain the reward that is promised to those who give only in the eyes of the Lord.

PUT IT IN THE PLATE

Giving to organizations and toward projects can be both exciting and rewarding. On the other hand, dropping the envelope in the collection each Sunday can seem mundane and even lack-luster. A sound system for the middle school ministry (as if they need help with amplification)? A gift to a missionary retirement home? Paying the utilities? Please! Let me put my money where it's going to yield a sweeter return. Yet Paul's instructions to the Corinthian believers bring it all back home again:

Now about the collection for God's people: Do what I told the
Galatian churches to do. On the first day of every week, each one
of you should set aside a sum of money in keeping with his income,
saving it up, so that when I come no collections will have to be made.
Then, when I arrive, I will give letters of introduction to the men
you approve and send them with your gift to Jerusalem.

—1 Corinthians 16:1–4

Certainly there is freedom to support parachurch organizations—through this book we will encourage you to do so.
However, as believers *we also have* a responsibility to support our
local church.

DON'T FORGET THE FAMILY

We will take a practical look at what this means in the next chapter,
but for now we simply want to stress the high priority God places
on meeting the physical needs of the family:

If anyone does not provide for his relatives, and especially for his
immediate family, he has denied the faith and is worse than an
unbeliever.

—1 Timothy 5:8

God has not left a lot of gray regarding the area of giving! Truth
will vary in application from family to family, but the standard

is clear. While our culture focuses on caring for our children and grandchildren, remember that in the Jewish culture, children (especially sons) were also charged with the care of their elderly parents. Ignoring either is unacceptable—bringing a harsh comparison that leaves the neglecting believer in an unenviable position in God's eyes.

Don't Take Our Word for It

We opened this chapter by looking at Scripture that described and defined our God as the ultimate giver. We then looked at selected passages that reflect God's values in giving—values that we should apply in our stewardship of His resources. Yet we have only begun to unfold the theology of giving.

There was much more we could say regarding each topic, but we intentionally chose to focus on the centerpieces of a biblical theology. This has come from our diligent search to understand God's Word. Now it's your turn.

Our challenge to you is to search God's Word for yourself—be like the Bereans, who even checked to see if the apostle Paul was going by the book! Our goal is simply to encourage you to continue to unfold the rich doctrines of our giving God and the great responsibilities of His stewards. Use the passages we provided as the starting point for your personal study, then expand it with the help of your concordance and commentaries.

And while self-discovery of truth is noble, be sure to discuss your discoveries with your accountability or Bible study partners.

Sound biblical theology isn't built on single verses, but on the truth that comes from understanding verses in context and comparing and contrasting similar passages.

We believe that as you search the heart of God you will grow to follow in His footsteps and give in a way that pleases Him.

"The ground of a certain rich man produced a good crop. He thought to himself, 'What shall I do? I have no place to store my crops.'

"Then he said, 'This is what I'll do. I will tear down my barns and build bigger ones, and there I will store all my grain and my goods. And I'll say to myself, "You have plenty of good things laid up for many years. Take life easy; eat, drink and be merry."'"

—*Luke 12:16–19*

As he looked up, Jesus saw the rich putting their gifts into the temple treasury. He also saw a poor widow put in two very small copper coins. "I tell you the truth," he said, "this poor widow has put in more than all the others. All these people gave their gifts out of their wealth; but she out of her poverty put in all she had to live on."

—*Luke 21:1–4*

CHAPTER FIVE

Sowing and Reaping

The two passages on page 75 highlight opposite ends of the spectrum in stewardship. They bring us back to the question: Who owns what? Today, by the world's standards most of those who read this book are positioned like the "rich man" while most of the world's population is like the poor widow. Will we who hold such incredible resources build bigger barns? Or will we boldly give in such a way that will stretch our level of comfort?

Paul addressed the subject of sowing and reaping in Galatians.

> *Do not be deceived: God cannot be mocked. A man reaps what he sows. The one who sows to please his sinful nature, from that nature will reap destruction; the one who sows to please the Spirit, from the Spirit will reap eternal life.*
>
> —*Galatians 6:7–8*

When it is all said and done, sowing and reaping are heart issues.

The Bible talks much about sowing and reaping because in early times the economy was intimately tied to agriculture and wealth was calculated in terms of livestock, land, and large families. Today we live in a dynamic and sometimes volatile economy, where economic swings can happen quickly.

Sowing and reaping today is much different from early times and is affected by influencers such as energy supplies, personal and government debt, terrorism, natural disasters, and geopolitical events. Nothing of the world and its riches is certain and nothing is permanent. Nonetheless, today we live in the most prosperous time of history and a big part of the reason is that many have developed a capability and capacity to build and accumulate wealth. Even the middle-class, with tools like 401(k)s, IRAs, and other retirement accounts, has the means to accumulate far more than earlier generations. Solomon with all his riches would be stunned by what he would see in our world today.

In the midst of these blessings and God's grace in our lives, how can we be good stewards and apply best practices for sowing and reaping? By learning about the planning tools that will allow us to sow for the purposes of growing and multiplying and reap for the purposes of giving and investing in God's kingdom.

Wealth management typically involves four professional disciplines: investment, tax, insurance, and legal. As Christians, we also believe planning should include the spiritual component that links our purpose and mission as good stewards. Our heart and our head should be in concert as we make decisions about our stewardship responsibilities.

Unfortunately, the average investor has at best a fragmented approach to wealth management—and perhaps worse, a haphazard plan of wealth transfer. The problem is that the individuals usually do not have the knowledge, awareness, or understanding of sophisticated planning tools or how these various disciplines need to work together. Even if they have a financial advisor, overall implementation and execution is done by a variety of individual professionals specializing in different areas—leading to a lack of integration and resulting in fragmented planning. The challenge is getting everyone on the same page to develop a holistic, comprehensive, integrated plan.

Integrated wealth management operates much like an orchestra. The conductor knows when to bring in the strings, the brass, the woodwinds, and the percussion. What distinguishes a "maestro" is his ability to bring the music alive. Likewise, a financial strategist who knows when and how to orchestrate all the various professional disciplines can help you leave a legacy of significance that has earthly and eternal impact.

Investment

In our practice we see people make decisions about their investment portfolio that can be kindly described as inefficient. They simply make bad investment decisions or invest in areas that do not suit them. Investment planning and management can be a sophisticated and complex navigational task. Some people collect investments like shoes in a closet. Some may be seasonal and others lack quality, but often they don't complement the wardrobe. Investments are sometimes chosen because of a catchy name, fancy marketing materials, or merely because someone else has it. When little or no due diligence is done, the investment rarely accomplishes the investor's goals.

It's also common for people to utilize a relationship they have with a broker to implement the investments, but then they have no system of management afterward. This is commonly called "passive investing." With volatility and increased risk in the markets due to geopolitical events such as terrorist attacks, energy crises, or acts of war, proactive management by a qualified management team is essential to protect the investors and reduce exposure to major downturns in their portfolio.

Investing can be divided into three categories—short term (in the one-to-five-year range), intermediate (in the five-to-ten-year range), and long term (beyond ten years). Short-term investing is usually about accumulating and keeping liquid a part of the portfolio that remains immediately accessible. Intermediate investing is usually targeted at specific objectives like buying a home or paying for a college education, and growth and risk is balanced with the timing of the need. Long-term investing is often focused on retirement with an objective of growth within the risk tolerance level of the investor.

Good investment planning for the long term must take into account the impact of taxes, inflation, and market risk. Tax implications for different savings and investment strategies can have a dramatic affect on the ultimate outcome of assets available at retirement. Likewise the impact of inflation must be considered. An investment strategy must keep up with and ideally exceed inflation. The markets regularly (and somewhat unpredictably) rise and fall. Over the long run it's not about "timing the market," it's about "managing market conditions." The amount of market risk that an individual takes must be correlated to individual risk tolerance.

It is essential that a portfolio design is structured before any implementation of new investments. If you were going to build a home you would logically start with an architectural drawing before beginning construction. The same is true with investing—it is critical to follow a plan. There are four major categories of investments that are universal to a comprehensive portfolio structure.

Category 1: *Emergency Reserve*—This category contains investments that are liquid and convenient. However, because this is normally a low-performing category it should not contain a significant amount of assets.

Category 2: *Non-Qualified Professionally Managed Accounts*— This category is also liquid and is meant to be used for investing in growth and income instruments for moderate-to-long-term planning. This category should be proactively managed by a professional team based on the individual's investment goals.

Category 3: *Qualified Professionally Managed Accounts*—This category involves investments that are tax advantaged and are primarily for retirement planning. Again the management of these assets is of key importance since they will eventually be used for retirement income throughout the individual's lifespan.

Category 4: *Real Property*—This category includes investments like a home, investment property, business, and other material possessions. These types of investments are not liquid but are common to the portfolio mix.

Most people have an imbalance between the four categories. It is quite common to have an overemphasis in categories 1 and 4. Prior to implementation of any investments, it is necessary to plan a specific strategy that will achieve the proper balance to meet the individual's financial objectives and goals.

The area of investment selection must be carefully considered, taking many variables into consideration. One area of investing that should be of importance to all Christians is the morally and socially conscious selection of investments within their portfolio. Unfortunately many corporations that issue stock are advancing their political agenda by supporting areas that are in direct conflict with a Christian's moral and social values. Management systems available today may automatically exclude investments that contradict a believer's values.

Contributions and compounding growth are factors that build assets over time. However, asset allocation and diversification are also key to sustaining long-term growth. Asset allocation is the process by which you spread your investment dollars over several categories of assets, usually referred to as asset classes. These classes include stocks, bonds, cash (and equivalents), real estate, precious metals, collectibles, and insurance products. Diversification refers to the more specific choices made within each asset class, for example in the asset class of stocks an investor may diversify into small cap, medium cap, or large cap stocks. The concept of diversification of a portfolio is very important, but also diversification of the management systems is essential.

Tax

The next professional discipline relates to the area of taxes. We have found that the vast majority of people are dissatisfied with the amount of taxes they pay each year and find this to be the most worrisome of the four disciplines. Most people have developed a relationship with an accountant or a CPA to prepare their taxes each year. This professional is an important member of your wealth management team. Professionals working in this discipline do tax preparation, tax filing, bookkeeping, and auditing, making sure the client stays in compliance with the regulations of the Internal Revenue Code. However, most clients rarely receive tax reduction planning advice from these professionals prior to filing their income tax returns. We have found that due to this missing component of the wealth management process, the majority of people pay excess taxes unnecessarily over their lifetime.

A good starting point is to find a qualified professional who specializes in tax-reduction planning and can conduct an audit of your prior three years of tax returns to determine if there were any missed deductions. This professional should be a compatible member of your wealth management team and does not replace your current accountant or CPA. The ultimate goal is to implement legitimate tax-reduction strategies to mitigate paying unnecessary taxes. While Matthew 22:21 reminds us that we are to "Give to Caesar what is Caesar's," a legitimate reduction of taxes is essential to being a wise steward.

Tax-reduction planning is focused on reducing, deferring, or in some cases, eliminating taxes. Some of the tools used to implement a tax-reduction strategy include:

- IRA
- Roth IRA
- 529 plans
- Tax-free bonds
- Life insurance
- Annuities
- Deferred compensation plans
- Pension and profit-sharing plans (401[k], 403[b])
- Estate freeze
- Welfare benefit trust (health only)
- Captive insurance companies

One strategy often used is "tax harvesting." Instead of focusing on one tax, tax harvesting considers all possible taxes, including estate, gift, capital gains, earned income, passive income, and alternative minimum taxes, each of which can impact the efficiency of the individual's wealth management plan.

Tax laws are constantly changing so it is imperative to regularly review the tax planning aspect of your wealth management plan. Tax planning is not optional; it is an essential requirement to maintaining good stewardship of the resources you have been entrusted with.

Insurance

Insurance is one of the most complex areas in the wealth management process, but also one of the most important. Because there are so many forms of insurance necessary to adequately protect the needs of an individual, the process requires a variety of specialists in the insurance arena. Most individuals have several different forms of insurance and have very little understanding of the terms of their insurance contracts, including coverage, exclusions, deductibles, expenses, and competitiveness. This is akin to looking at your homeowner's policy after your house burns down, only to discover you didn't have the coverage you thought you had.

The following is a list of the various types of insurance that are important in a comprehensive insurance portfolio of a wealth management plan.

- Life insurance
- Disability income insurance
- Health insurance

- Long-term care insurance
- Homeowner's insurance
- Vehicle insurance
- Umbrella liability insurance
- Business or professional insurance

Because the insurance industry is constantly evolving and changing, it is important that the key financial strategist mentioned earlier has an adequate understanding of each of the required components of the insurance portfolio and does regular reviews with the insurance professionals on the wealth management team. Since everything we have been given comes with a stewardship responsibility, the area of insurance planning plays an integral part in preserving and protecting the resources God has blessed us with.

Legal

Legal planning is the process of developing and implementing a comprehensive plan for the effective and orderly disposition of assets during your lifetime and at death. Legal planning is a complex process that covers many areas, such as wills, trusts, health-care directives, powers of attorney, guardianship selection, charitable planned giving, design of legal entities, and business continuation plans. It is one of the most important areas of wealth management, and it is not unique to economic status. Proper legal planning can influence the futures of a spouse, children, grandchildren, and other heirs as well as have an impact for the kingdom by funding charitable organizations. If there are substantial assets, making a long-term legal plan is not merely an option—it is a necessity. A well-developed plan offers an opportunity to leave behind a lasting legacy that will impact family and perhaps others for eternity.

A key strategy in legal planning and positioning assets for distribution and wealth transfer involves the utilization of trusts and legal entities. While we can offer a general overview of various trusts and what they are, putting them into play requires investment, legal, tax, and insurance expertise. This is why it is imperative to orchestrate a comprehensive and integrated strategy so that all these disciplines are working together to deliver a wealth management plan that meets the individual's holistic goals. The following are examples of wealth management tools that are often used to help accomplish the financial goals of a good steward.

Testamentary Trust

A testamentary trust is one that is created and funded under the terms of your will. It does not come into existence until your death. Assets that are transferred to the trust must pass through probate. Until your death, you can change the terms of the trust by amending your will. Upon your death, the trust becomes irrevocable. A testamentary trust can be contingent. That means that it will be created upon your death only if certain conditions are present (e.g., your children are under a certain age).

LIVING TRUST

A living trust, also called an *inter vivos* trust, is created while you are living. A living trust can either end or continue at your death. Property in the trust is distributed according to the terms of the trust, not your will. Living trust assets avoid probate.

REVOCABLE TRUST

As the name implies, you can revoke or amend the terms of a revocable trust. You can change the beneficiaries or trustee. You can add or remove assets from the trust. You can also change the provisions of the trust. You can even dissolve the trust. Furthermore, at your death, the assets in the revocable trust do not pass by the terms of your will (and thus do not pass through probate). Instead, the assets in a revocable trust are distributed in accordance with the terms of the trust. Many people set up a revocable living trust simply to avoid the delay and cost of probate. However, one big disadvantage to a revocable trust is that the assets in the trust will be included in your gross estate for estate tax purposes. Thus, a revocable trust is not used to avoid estate taxes. *Caution:* A revocable trust may become an irrevocable trust at the death of the grantor, unless the grantor gives someone else the power to amend the trust. The spouse of the decedent, for example, cannot change the terms of the trust unless he or she is given a special power of appointment.

IRREVOCABLE TRUST

Again, as the name implies, an irrevocable trust is one that you cannot revoke or amend once the trust has been established. This means that you cannot dissolve the trust, change the beneficiaries, remove assets from the trust, or change the terms of the trust. The main advantage to setting up an irrevocable trust is that the assets in the trust, including any future appreciation, are not included in your gross estate for estate tax purposes. Of course, the transfer to an irrevocable trust may be a taxable gift, and gift taxes may have to be paid at the time of the transfer. A secondary benefit of an irrevocable trust may be that the assets in the trust are beyond the reach of your creditors. Irrevocable trusts are used primarily as estate planning tools. With careful planning, you may be able to save substantial amounts in estate taxes. There are many different types of irrevocable trusts. They include (among others) an irrevocable life insurance trust (to hold an insurance policy), a qualified personal residence trust (to hold a personal residence), and a grantor retained annuity trust (to provide you with income).

Outright Gift

In the typical situation, a gift is for the charitable organization's benefit only, and the charity will take possession of the gift immediately. This type of gift is called an outright gift. This arrangement satisfies the general rule that a gift to charity must be paid to the charity in the form of money or property before the end of the tax year to be deductible for income tax purposes.

Split Interest Gift in Trust

Another option is for your gift to be split between a charity and a noncharitable beneficiary. This is called a "split interest gift in trust." Here, one party (usually the noncharitable beneficiary) receives the use of the donated property for a specific period of time, which means he or she is paid a certain sum every year out of the donated property. Then after this time period is up, the remaining property passes to the charity. Such gifts can be used to provide for a dependent child or a surviving spouse. In this arrangement, the charity's right to enjoyment and possession of the gift is delayed because the noncharitable beneficiary has the first interest in the donated property. Ordinarily, this delay would mean no tax deductibility for your gift. However, Congress has voiced its approval of such arrangements as long as the gift is set up as one of a number of special trusts expressly created for this purpose. If your split interest gift is set up as one of these trusts, you receive federal income, gift, and estate tax deductions.

CHARITABLE REMAINDER TRUST

A charitable remainder trust should be considered if you own assets (investment property, stocks, mutual funds, or a business) that have appreciated over their cost. This type of trust allows the donor to sell an asset that normally would be exposed to capital gain taxes and gift the asset to the trust and not defer the capital gains but eliminate them entirely. It also creates a tax deduction based on government tables and can provide a stream of income for the donor or beneficiaries for life. The following are examples of some of the varieties of charitable remainder trusts.

CHARITABLE REMAINDER ANNUITY TRUST—CRAT

A CRAT is a split interest gift between a noncharitable beneficiary and a charitable beneficiary. The noncharitable beneficiary has the first interest and the charity has the remainder interest or second-in-line interest. The trust pays out a fixed amount of income every year (an annuity) to the noncharitable beneficiary for the term of the trust and the remaining assets pass to the charity at the end of the term of the trust.

CHARITABLE REMAINDER UNITRUST—CRUT

A CRUT is a split interest gift between a noncharitable beneficiary and a charitable beneficiary. As with a CRAT, the noncharitable beneficiary has the first interest and the charity has the remainder interest. However, instead of paying out a fixed amount every year, a CRUT pays the noncharitable beneficiary a fluctuating amount each year, depending on the value of the trust assets for that year. This amount is calculated as a percentage of the assets in the trust on a specific date each year. At the end of the term of the trust, the remaining assets pass to the charity.

CHARITABLE LEAD TRUST—CLT

A CLT is a split interest gift between a noncharitable beneficiary and a charitable beneficiary. Here, the charity has the first or lead interest and the noncharitable beneficiary has the remainder interest. The charity is paid a certain amount every year for the term of the trust, and then the remaining assets pass to the noncharitable beneficiary at the end of the trust term.

POOLED INCOME FUND

A pooled income fund is a split interest gift between a noncharitable beneficiary and a charitable beneficiary. Like the CRAT and CRUT, the noncharitable beneficiary has the first interest and the charity has the remaining interest. A pooled income fund is managed by the charity (much like a mutual fund) and is made up of donations from several donors. The charity pays the noncharitable beneficiary a fluctuating amount each year, depending on the value of the fund in that year. These income distributions are made to the noncharitable beneficiary for his or her lifetime, after which the portion of the fund assets attributable to the noncharitable beneficiary is severed from the fund and used by the charity for its charitable purposes.

BARGAIN SALE

A bargain sale in the context of charitable giving is a sale to a charity at a bargain price (i.e., a price below the fair market value of the item sold, fair market value being the price a willing buyer would pay a willing seller in an arm's length transaction). The difference between the sale price and the actual fair market value of the asset equals your donation to charity. A bargain sale involves two separate transactions for tax purposes: a sale and a charitable gift. The IRS treats each event as a separate transaction. Consequently, each is reported separately on your income tax return.

PRIVATE FOUNDATION

Donors with sufficient resources may want to create a private foundation. A private foundation is a separate legal entity (often named for the donor) that can endure for many generations after the original donor's death. The donor creates the foundation, then transfers assets (typically appreciated assets) to the foundation, which in turn makes grants to public charities. The donor and his or her descendants retain complete control over which charities receive grants.

COMMUNITY FOUNDATION

A type of organization related to a private foundation is called a community foundation. A community foundation concentrates its activities within a defined geographic area and is typically controlled by a representative group of community members, which may include the donor. In practice, a community foundation is a public charity, though it appears to share some of the characteristics of a private foundation.

DONOR ADVISED FUNDS

Similar in some respects to a private foundation, a donor advised fund (DAF) offers an easy way for a donor to make significant charitable gifts over a long period of time. A DAF actually refers to an account that is held within a charitable organization. The charitable organization is a separate legal entity, but the donor's account is not—it is merely a component of the charitable organization that holds the account. Once the donor has transferred assets to the account, the charitable organization becomes the legal owner of the assets and has ultimate control over it. The donor can only advise—not direct—the charitable organization on how the donor's contributions will be distributed.

LIMITED LIABILITY COMPANY—LLC

An LLC is a hybrid of a general partnership and a C corporation. Like a partnership, income and tax liabilities pass through to the members, and the LLC is not double-taxed as a separate entity. And, like a C corporation, an LLC is considered a separate legal entity that can be used to own business assets and incur debt, protecting your personal assets from other nontax claims against the LLC.

FAMILY LIMITED PARTNERSHIP—FLP

An FLP is a limited liability partnership formed by family members only. At least one family member is a general partner; the others are limited partners. A creditor can't obtain a judgment against the FLP—it can only obtain a charging order. The charging order only allows the creditor to receive any income distributed by the general partner. It does not allow the creditor access to the assets of the FLP. Thus, a charging order is not an attractive remedy to most creditors. As a result, the limitation to seeking a charging order can often convince a creditor to settle on more reasonable terms than might otherwise be possible.

It is not realistic for us to provide the entire range of options or a comprehensive list of all the financial-planning tools available. Depending on your net worth, planning and execution can be a sophisticated and complex task. Most people's assets are not properly protected. In what may be a well-meaning effort, they allow children to be beneficiaries of large inheritances and end up disabling their offspring. Perhaps the most inefficient aspect of all is their failure to plan properly. Most people don't plan to fail, they fail to plan. As a result, their negligence allows large amounts of their wealth to pass quietly and sometimes unnecessarily to the government in the form of taxes.

Where Do I Start?

The first step in the wealth management process is defining and clarifying individual goals, objectives, risk tolerance, income needs, and investment time horizons. Step two is designing a strategy for the portfolio that includes asset allocation, investment selection, manager selection, estate, and asset-protection planning tools. Step three is implementing and proactively managing the strategy. Finally, it is critical to continually monitor the portfolio and make adjustments to the strategy whenever necessary in order to meet the dynamic goals and objectives.

Many people find it extremely helpful to invest in a formal *written* financial plan. These plans can range from simple to extremely complex. One of the main benefits of having a written financial plan is that it can help you balance competing financial priorities. A written financial plan will clearly show you how your financial goals are related—for example, how saving for your children's college education might impact your ability to save for retirement. Then you can use the information you've gleaned to decide how to prioritize your goals, implement specific strategies, and choose suitable options and services. Most importantly, a written financial plan will allow you and your wealth advisor to conduct probability analysis studies that will enable you to look at the "what if" scenarios and ultimately address the question, "When is enough, enough?"

Wealth Management Cycle

As we go about managing and stewarding our wealth, it is important to understand how we pass through the various stages of the Wealth Management Cycle—see figure.

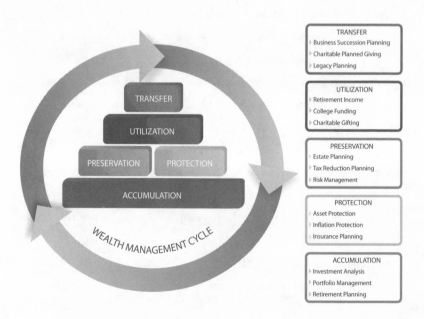

Stage 1—*Wealth Accumulation*

During the *wealth accumulation* stage the concentration is on saving, investing, and planning.

Stage 2—*Wealth Preservation*

During the *wealth preservation* stage the focus is on estate planning, tax-reduction planning, and risk management.

Stage 3—*Wealth Protection*

During the *wealth protection* stage it is important to zero in on asset-protection considerations, inflation protection, and insurance planning.

Stage 4—*Wealth Utilization*

During the *wealth utilization* stage it is all about beginning to use your investments for retirement income, college funding, and charitable gifting.

Stage 5—*Wealth Transfer*

During the *wealth transfer* stage the focus becomes charitable planned giving, legacy planning, and business-succession planning.

At different times in our lives we will concentrate and focus on different stages within the Wealth Management Cycle based on circumstances and our evolving wealth management plan. Remember that stewardship takes hard work and involves planning. Take your responsibility seriously and remember: "To whom much is given, much is expected."

The Most Important Goal

Earlier in this chapter we contrasted two people who made a decision about what to do with what they had: one with very much, one with very little. Many of us have reached a season of life where the seeds of God's blessings have reaped a harvest far beyond what we need. But how do we know what enough is and when enough is enough? When we fall prey to material aspirations or even the lure of material security, a vision of accumulated wealth can impede our character and spiritual formation. The parable of the rich

YOUR WEALTH MISSION STATEMENT

Don't get bogged down in the details so deeply that you forget why you're giving in the first place. One way to stay focused is to create and refer often to a personal "Wealth Mission Statement," a document that includes all the big-picture issues, including your theology of giving, as well as the evolving details of your giving plan. We've provided an outline in the Appendix of this book. Use it as a guide to create your own personal Wealth Mission Statement, and then use this as a dynamic living plan. Follow it, adjust it, and above all, let your family and heirs know about it so that your plan will continue to be carried out even after your death.

fool makes it clear that our time on this earth is temporal. While it is wise to make plans for our future, we need to always remember who is in control of that future: the very God who grants us the harvest.

NOW IT IS REQUIRED THAT THOSE WHO HAVE
BEEN GIVEN A TRUST MUST PROVE FAITHFUL.

—1 Corinthians 4:2

CHAPTER SIX

Investing in Blue-chip Ministries

—

Considering the term came out of the gambling world, it may seem irreverent to describe ministries as "blue chip." The blue chip was deemed the most valuable at the gaming table, and from there, the term shifted to the stock market where it is still used today as the hallmark of highest value.

We use the term to describe ministries that, like stocks, have established a track record of producing positive long-term returns for the kingdom. We understand that every organization will experience tests and transitions, but over the long run, a blue-chip ministry is far from a gamble. These are the ministries God has led us to invest in over the years.

By now we have built a foundation for the important concept that wise giving is more than a mere donation—it is truly an investment in God's kingdom. And as with any investment, we begin by doing the legwork—no small task when you consider there are more than ten thousand Christian nonprofit organizations in the United States alone!

Giving with Your Heart and Your Head

Investors are often dispassionate when choosing where to put their money. That is not to say that they do not consider moral and ethical issues in relation to the target company, but history shows that even those boundaries are often crossed. If their legwork turns up a winner they will remain with the company as long as it is profitable. If the stock starts to slide, well, let's just say that loyalty rarely extends beyond the bottom line. This is the way the world has done business for centuries.

Investing in God's kingdom, however, involves much more than acumen and occasional good luck. As we have said before, it is very much an issue of the heart. Over the years God has fanned a passion in our hearts and has led us to specifically invest in those ministries that not only share our passion, but also have translated it into results for the kingdom.

We remember one cool evening in Anaheim Stadium. We both felt goose bumps as we watched thousands of people answering Pastor Greg Laurie's invitation at a Harvest Crusade. They filed down the aisles like ants in response to the pure and simple message of the gospel. Evangelism was always important to us because we knew that apart from it we never would have had the opportunity to hear and believe the message of God's saving grace. But on this night, by witnessing the impact of the spoken word on so many lives, God fine-tuned our focus to fund evangelistic outreaches here at home and around the world.

That seed was nurtured through a foundation we formed in the early days of our stewardship journey. From the beginning we knew we needed counsel from mature, godly men and women, so we selected several to serve on the board. They helped us evaluate and select the ministries and causes to support, and together we saw God increase our investment for His glory. This experience only deepened our passion for evangelism. From reluctant giving on through obedient and joyful giving, finally we were entering the realm of *passionate* giving that God had prepared for us.

Since then we have worked to align ourselves with organizations that effectively share the gospel—in essence, those that generate a measurable rate of return. As an investor with a balanced portfolio, we support a wide diversity of evangelistic ministries around the world that employ varied strategies. What they all have in common is this bottom line: *transforming lives through the gospel.*

We should clarify that giving with the heart means more than spontaneous acts of generosity, which are often borne out of emotion. Many give in this manner, and they will be rewarded for doing so. (See Matt. 25:31–40, 10:42; 1 John 3:16–18.) But we are talking about something different. We're talking about allowing your heart to be seized by a God-given passion and giving yourself and your resources to see that passion bring forth light and life to this world. We constantly challenge ourselves to live lives that reflect the God-implanted passion for evangelism. And, if He hasn't already, we challenge you to allow Him to seize your heart with a passion that will touch the world—His world.

What is God passionate about? He's passionate about life. If you are too, then you ought to seek out the many good right-to-life ministries that are helping turn reluctant women into loving mothers and fetuses into tiny gifts to the world. God's also passionate about justice. If you are too, look for ministries that are fighting the horrors of the worldwide sex-trafficking industry or working to obtain the release of Christians imprisoned for their faith. He's passionate about relieving the suffering of the poor. If you are too, then align yourself with ministries that not only provide food and shelter to the impoverished of the world, but also teach them how to survive in their own environments. Search God's Word, find out what He treasures. You will discover what He loves, and you will come to love those same things. But be careful. You are stepping into a zone of passionate living and giving that will forever change your life.

It did ours.

What's Next?

As you search the Scriptures, pray, and seek advice, your heart may go in a hundred directions, but remember, your limited resources can't go there with you. God knows you can't meet every need, but He wants you to meet some specific ones. Ask Him to begin to narrow down the possibilities (James 1:5–6).

In your search for your philanthropic passion, we encourage you to answer questions like, "What do you believe God wants you to achieve?" "What problem do you want to help solve?" "What evil do you want to help correct?" or even, "What group of people do you want to see reached?" The answers don't come overnight, but in time God lifts the fog and reveals His heart's desire for each person, couple, or family.

Once the "what" becomes clear, it's time to begin the legwork and find that organization or those organizations most likely to share and achieve the passion God has instilled in you. Prayer, discussion, and sound advice are important steps in the process, but God also uses other methods. God used our years of exposure to the investment world to help us find "blue-chip" ministries.

Common Threads

There are many similarities between the components of blue-chip ministries and blue-chip corporations. We list some of these common threads here, realizing that there are many other worthy examples. As you continue to seek His guidance you will certainly find ministries that hold many of these values and follow many of these practices.

Let's not forget that our God is a strategic God. For centuries the business world has been using His principles, often far more effectively than the church. It's time we start applying His principles to the stewardship of His resources wherever applicable!

LEADERSHIP

We expect to find leaders who are focused on a clear mission statement and who have a bold vision to accomplish that mission. They must be godly, passionate, and always emit a sense of urgency for the task. They must be dedicated and educated, yet have the practical know-how to move smoothly from the abstract to the concrete. We believe that you must have the right people at the core, people who are committed to the ministry's purposes. They must be able to communicate the purposes well and clearly respect the expectations and standards of those who invest in the ministry.

One of the most important qualities of a great leader is to be a servant leader. We've had the privilege of personally knowing one of those very unique individuals—Dr. Sam Metcalf the president and one of the founders of Church Resource Ministries (CRM). Over the past three decades Sam has pioneered the strategic development and growth of CRM to engage and empower leaders in more than twenty-five countries across the world. Sam uses his gifts of wisdom and discernment to identify future leaders by seeing them through God's eyes and then empowering them through encouragement and mentoring to go out and change the world using their own personal leadership gifts. A leader of leaders yet always a servant excelling in humility.

A great leader is one who has identified and is willing to live according to God's plan and call on his or her life. Doug Mazza, the president of the international disability outreach ministry Joni and Friends, made a life-changing decision when he left his top American executive position as the chief operating officer for

Hyundai Motor America and answered the call to lead in full-time Christian ministry. Seeing that God had prepared him in advance for this unique leadership role through many of his personal life experiences, including raising a son with disabilities, Doug followed the call and leads with strength and passion. A leader who is confident he is fulfilling the purpose for which God created him is an inspiration to all.

Great leaders can inspire others by their vision. Rick Warren epitomizes such leadership. As a young man in his twenties, he set out to plant a church in Southern California. Beginning with a few people in his living room he launched Saddleback Church with a vision of ministering to thousands. Back then he even described a campus setting that is very much like the Saddleback Church of today, a church that rests on several acres and ministers to over twenty thousand people. His expansive vision is not about how big he can dream but how big is his God. Today the scope of his vision is literally the world, believing that God's work through churches big and small can address the problems of spiritual darkness, leadership, disease, education, and poverty by mobilizing believers to actively engage with those who are lost.

Leadership involves sacrifice. Bruce Smith, CEO of Wycliffe Associates, the support arm of Wycliffe Bible Translators, is one of the most talented, creative, and gifted leaders we know. Bruce would command a much higher salary in the corporate sector given his gifts and talents but has "sacrificed" the financial path and chosen to use his leadership skills to run this large organization that spans the globe. Bruce is a perfect example of what Jim Collins calls a "level five leader" in his book *Good to Great*. He is a perfect blend of humility and fierce resolve that exemplifies self-sacrifice for the higher cause.

Another mark of a great leader is humility. Chuck Colson, once one of the most powerful men in American politics, was stripped of power and position and served time in prison for his part in the Watergate scandal. Prior to his imprisonment he humbled himself before God and acknowledged that he was hopelessly lost and needed the saving power of a loving God. Perhaps he could have avoided a prison sentence by plea-bargaining and making a deal, but instead he did not waver: He faced the consequences and went to prison. After serving his time he launched a ministry to reach out to the incarcerated. Today, Prison Fellowship showcases God's love and transformational power by reaching prisoners and their families with the life-changing message of the gospel.

EFFICIENCY AND EFFECTIVENESS

There are different measuring sticks for ministry efficiency. One of the most common is the percentage of income used by the organization for overhead and fund-raising. Obviously, the lower the percentage used in the home office, the more resources available in the field. Many organizations earmark 15–20 percent for these purposes, and exact figures can be obtained from an organization on request.

Another perspective of efficiency is demonstrated by publishing house David C. Cook and its overseas division, Cook International. For more than 130 years the U.S.-based company has been a leading publisher of Sunday school curriculum, commentaries, and children's Bibles. Instead of simply turning profits to dividends, however, the home-base division fully funds and fuels the international outreach division. First, it has translated many books and commentaries into more than two hundred foreign languages, with authors granting royalty-free rights for their works. Second, David C. Cook pays all administrative overhead for Cook International, so every dollar invested delivers a dollar's worth of evangelism and discipleship resources to grassroots pastors and leaders around the world. Not all ministries can structure themselves in this way, but Cook's level of efficiency is a model for others to follow.

The Far East Broadcasting Company (FEBC) has been bringing "Christ to the World by Radio" for more than sixty years. It reaches into the homes of countless millions through broadcasts in 150 languages. Billy Graham has cited FEBC as one of the most effective and consistent voices in Christianity. Of course this is wonderful for those where electricity or batteries are readily available, but it means little to those who live in the villages and barrios where fires still provide the only light in the home each night. Realizing this problem, FEBC has distributed tens of thousands of crank-powered and conventional radios around the world, allowing people without access to electricity or expensive batteries to daily hear the gospel. This is an excellent example of using human technology for God's glory. FEBC is an efficient and effective ministry reaching millions daily across impenetrable borders.

One of our personal favorites in the area of efficiency and effectiveness is a ministry called Fellowship of Christian Athletes (FCA).

Sports are a great attraction for the young. So many life lessons can be learned when participating in sports programs, from leadership to sacrifice to discipline. One of the ways FCA reaches out to the youth is by offering comprehensive athletic, spiritual, and leadership training in a camp setting. Our daughter Erika attended one of those FCA camps and returned home not quite the same Erika. She was changed by the worship experience and the words of the speakers and was challenged to think about what it really means to give her life to Christ. During that camp her faith became her own. After camp she determined how she could live and show her faith in her sport and to this day, before every race she runs, she meditates on how she can compete to show God's glory. Close to fifty thousand kids attended FCA camps this last summer. Efficient AND effective.

Innovation

If Plato was correct in saying that necessity is the mother of invention, then it also must be a close relative to innovation.

One of the more innovative organizations we've discovered is Church Resource Ministries (CRM). As we mentioned CRM's mission is to develop and empower leaders who can lead healthy, growing churches around the world. One of the ways CRM sustains its ministry as it expands to developing countries around the world is to utilize the integrity of the business model to provide profit to allow such ministries to emerge and thrive. This method is called Enterprise International.

A concrete example of this is CRM's work in Romania. In the

early 1990s a businessman from Orange County, California, Jeri Little, moved, along with his family, to the remote city of Iaşi to join the CRM ministry team there. Though the Littles were full-time missionaries, their specific work was to build a profitable business that could sustain long-term ministry in Romania. Today, the enterprises begun by the Littles, including a restaurant-hotel complex called Little Texas, and a Romanian-owned real estate development firm, provide upwards of five hundred thousand dollars annually to support a wide range of ministry in Romania.

Hope International is another great innovator. Hope International ministers to the poor in over a dozen countries in a very unique way. Founder Jeff Rutt, a nationally known custom homebuilder, was motivated to help in a way that offered longer-lasting benefits than those provided by short-term charitable giving. His premise was that many intelligent, ambitious would-be entrepreneurs around the world have the savvy, but lack the capital, to start their businesses. Hope International began to provide microfinancing to help people break from financial entrapment and move from poverty to provision to the reality of starting a business and becoming self-sufficient. Hope International's success has been phenomenal, realizing a repayment rate of 99 percent. Most importantly, the hope of the gospel is shared in the context of these relationships, ministering to spiritual poverty as well.

SYNERGY

Short of a full-on merger, synergy allows for two or more entities to work together to accomplish more than each could separately.

Today mission agencies and ministry organizations are joining their resources and expertise to save time and money, while more effectively reaching ministry goals that would take years to reach on their own.

Wycliffe Associates' strategy, involving volunteers in the advancement of Bible translation, harnesses the synergy of tens of thousands of Christians using their God-given gifts. Rather than asking men and women to become something they are not, Wycliffe Associates asks them to use the very skills and experience God has invested in their lives as part of a global team, speeding Scripture into every language. Accountants, computer technicians, teachers, carpenters, and even financial consultants perform vital tasks that increase the impact of linguistic teams doing the translation work. Without these professionals Bible translation slows as people are forced to work outside their area of expertise. The Wycliffe Associates team reflects the synergy God intended for the body of Christ. During 2007, some 1,341 Wycliffe Associates volunteers served in thirty-five countries worldwide. Their growth goal is to involve more than five thousand volunteers each year in advancing Bible translation.

Open Doors began its ministry in 1955, with Brother Andrew, who is a native of Holland. Brother Andrew recounts the beginnings in his book, titled *God's Smuggler*, which describes how he went behind the Iron Curtain to deliver Bibles: "It's important to note that in those days having a Bible could be a life and death proposition." Today with the support of thousands of volunteers, the work of Open Doors reaches areas of limited access around the world—places where people following Christ can pay the ultimate price with their lives. Open Doors provides Bible and literature distribution, leadership training, and Christian community development. Open Doors USA is led by Dr. Carl Moeller, who leads with the focus on prayer, presence, and advocacy, encouraging believers to pray fervently for those who are suffering, to make personal visits to the persecuted who are part of the Christian family, and to be advocates speaking up for those who may have no voice.

These are just a few of the common threads we have recognized in our blue-chip ministries. These values are important for success in ministry or business. Common denominators like these are helpful, but they are only the first step in discovering blue-chip ministries. With all the available options today, your homework is just beginning, but that's another similarity between the stock market and the ministry world.

Six Steps to Finding Blue-Chip Ministries

1. REVIEW MARKETING MATERIAL AND FINANCIALS

Modern ministries dwell under a banner with the adage "Publish or Perish," so obtaining written and electronically accessed information about any one of them is an easy first step. Brochures and other collateral material (videos, PowerPoint presentations, etc.) will be delivered free on request by most ministries. Study and watch these closely to familiarize yourself with the information available at this introductory level. Likewise, log on to the Web site and dig deeper than the home page into the organization's history, endorsements, and staff backgrounds.

Be careful, though, not to judge a book solely by its cover. Some organizations are long on sizzle, as one mission leader calls it, and short on substance. It's easy to put together a stunning brochure and Web site, but not always easy to live up to the claims made in them. And conversely, the ministry with a misspelled word on the back cover of its brochure may be outproducing the one with the pretty pictures and perfect punctuation. Your subsequent investigation will help to further sort through this information jam and separate the blue chips from the rest of the field.

Along with the organization-generated material, be sure to request its annual report and Form 990 from the home office. They provide detailed accounting of the organization's financial status over the last fiscal year—and can be extremely helpful if you take the time to study them closely.

Several entities help donors evaluate an organization's fiscal responsibility. By selecting member organizations on the basis of strict criteria involving independent annual audits and/or reviews, these entities provide a stamp of approval on those groups that meet the high standards of Christian stewardship. Two of the oldest and most respected of the accreditation agencies are the Evangelical Council for Fiscal Accountability (ECFA) and The Mission Exchange (formerly the EFMA, or Evangelical Fellowship of Mission Agencies). Membership in either of these should be a prerequisite for any ministry you give to.

Very informative resources to use when evaluating a ministry can be found online at www.MinistryWatch.com or www.GuideStar.org. The Better Business Bureau's Wise Giving Alliance is also an excellent source of information.

All of these resources, however, do not eliminate the need for prayer. God is not playing shell games—He really does have a special place for His resources, and He really wants to lead you to that place. So do the legwork, but make sure you spend time on your knees as well.

2. ASSESS GOALS AND STRATEGIES

The next stage involves taking a closer look at the clearly stated vision and mission statements God has used to touch and excite your heart.

Many of these statements may sound similar on the surface so you need to discover what, if anything, makes an organization unique. This may be its geographic or expansive reach, its ability to access difficult areas of the world, or its innovative methodologies.

From the vision and mission statement flows the means of accomplishing the organization's goals—a functioning strategy statement. An organization should have a three-to-five-year plan in place and evaluate and adjust this plan on a regular basis. It should come as no surprise that many ministries and missions use a business model, including backward mapping, to accomplish ministry goals. While many are "in-house" documents, any organization striving to be transparent should be able to provide this information in a general format. Evaluate the organization's processes in light of its stated goals to see if both are reasonable and if the former can achieve the latter. Don't hesitate to ask questions. Is there sufficient infrastructure to provide capability and capacity? How does it generate support to meet its goals?

If the goals and strategies of the organization have permeated its personnel, then people at every level should be able to quickly and clearly articulate both. If they cannot, then be aware of a critical missing link in the organization's ethos.

Goals and strategies typically establish what an organization wants to accomplish—but business and ministry alike need to deal with the realities of everyday life, including problem solving. Ask the ministry's representative to share some of the problems it is facing (beyond finances) and how it is attempting to resolve them. What processes are used? Who gets involved, and at what level? Which (if any) problems are long-standing? Beyond the expectation of handling them in a godly manner, how an organization solves problems demonstrates its flexibility and ingenuity in the pressure cooker of ministry.

3. GET TO KNOW LEADERSHIP

We have already addressed the general issue of leadership but here we want to list some specific areas to examine. This level of inquiry will require more effort than the previous two. It will likely involve a personal visit—and probably more than one—with the organization's executive leadership. We're talking about seeing leadership in action, either in a ministry context locally or even in a mission context overseas.

Here are some key areas to discern through observation or direct inquiry:

- How do leaders lead? Do they employ a collaborative style, or a "command and control" style of leadership?
- How well does the leadership communicate vision?
- What are the qualifications and experience of leadership? Has there been evidence of producing results in the leaders' past endeavors?
- What are the qualifications and experience of the board of directors? Do its members understand their roles and responsibilities? Do they provide accountability to the leadership, and are they financially committed to the organization?
- Last, and certainly not least, are they godly men and women? God's expectations of leaders in 1 Timothy 3 and Titus 1 can be applied in most ministry leadership contexts. And Christ's admonition to the apostles in Matthew 20:26–27 should be woven into every leader's life: "Whoever wants to become great among you must be your servant, and whoever wants to be first must be your slave." Pride has ruined executive officers from Satan to megachurch pastors to mission leaders. Pride may be an admired prerequisite to success in the business world, but any hint of it among ministry leaders should send you for the door.

Often ministries host "donor events." These are typically structured as a weekend conference where the organization is well represented. Attending one of these events is an excellent way to get to know the leadership and to evaluate the efficiency and effectiveness of the organization.

One note of care … while it may be ideal to meet and get to know the CEO or CFO, realize that the top leaders may not be the most accessible. If the leadership team is functioning in a cohesive manner, the ethos should be readily discerned at any level—connect where you can.

4. Evaluate Results

Getting things done is the hallmark of a steward, and it should be the hallmark of any ministry that is given stewardship of the gospel. Like the business world, good intentions don't count (Matt. 21:28–30).

Effectiveness, however, can be evaluated by a variety of metrics. Starting with the mission and strategy statements, each organization or agency should have a means by which it measures results and outcomes of its ministry. While well-established organizations have built well-earned reputations for producing desired results, many newer and smaller organizations employ business models to determine and assess their progress. These obviously help to reach their goals, but they also provide a sense of security for potential investors in their ministry.

The turn of the millennium provided impetus for many Christian organizations to reassess, refocus, and in many cases relabel themselves. For some it was merely a fresh coat of paint, but others made significant adjustments to what they did, how they did it, and for some, with whom they did it. As a result of this, many set goals ten, twenty, and even twenty-five years in the future, meaning now is an excellent time to assess how they are doing in light of their projections. Consider mitigating circumstances (the world has changed much even in this short period) yet graciously evaluate their performance—and ask members of the leadership team to do the same. Realize that at this stage they are not accountable to you, but their response should be circumspect if they want the type of reciprocal and transparent relationship so integral to ministry partnership.

You will find that most ministries and missions are comprised of the highest quality of people who seek to walk in the light of the Lord. Yet, similar to our previous warning, beware of extravagant claims backed only by anecdotal evidence. Paul wrote in Philippians 4:8: "Finally, brothers, whatever is true, whatever is noble, whatever is right, whatever is pure, whatever is lovely, whatever is admirable— if anything is excellent or praiseworthy—think about such things." The benefit of the doubt that stems from being in Christ should be extended to all Christians. Yet Christ said that many will do mighty works in His name—and He will tell them "I never knew you." Do your homework, but also ask Him for discernment to help you invest in ministries with proven track records.

5. LEARN THE CULTURE

The first endeavor of any missionary who hopes to reach a group of people with the gospel is to learn its language and culture. As investors of God's resources, it behooves us to do the same.

Whether they recognize it or not, whether planned or not, every organization has its own culture. The more established the organization, the more dominant the culture. Many of the most prominent mission organizations were formed shortly after the end of WW II. We know that the culture, or outward behavior, of any group is merely a by-product of its values. Therefore, it's important to open new doors in order to enter this inner realm of the organization.

Along with vision, mission, and strategy statements, a ministry should have a set of written values that are central to what it does and how it does it. These should affect every area of its ministry, from how it treats employees and volunteers to its commitment to ongoing learning for its members. Like a family, one staff member should be able to finish the sentence of another in regard to ministry matters. Staff members of a blue-chip organization function and sacrifice together for the common goal apart from outside directives. They will all, without hesitation, tell you they are part of accomplishing something very near and dear to the heart of God.

Here are a few things you, as the investor, ought to consider about the organization:

- Its values pertaining to ethical, fiscal, and legal compliance.
- Its values regarding feedback and accountability to you.
- Its transparency relative to problems, successes, and failures.

- Its openness to develop synergistic relationships with like-minded ministries.

The values of the organization should permeate its leadership structure, its personnel, its goals, and its methodologies. If they do then it will be apparent, in one way or another, in most everything they accomplish.

6. PROBE PROJECTS

Giving to ministries can take on many forms, but one of the most attractive is the "ministry project." A ministry project is defined, measurable, has a beginning and an end, and well, it feels good. Whether this means funding a Bible translation or a microenterprise bank, projects often provide the bang for the buck that many investors seek.

As appealing and needed as projects are, even the most pure can become a Bermuda Triangle if not properly planned and managed. And here is another warning: As in any charitable context, from 9/11 to tsunami relief, some present-day "projects" are little more than snake oil "remedies" pitched by descendants of nineteenth-century elixir peddlers.

Christ used building and planning concepts in many of His parables. (See especially Luke 6:48–49 Matt. 7:24–27.) In Luke 14:25–33 He explains that the wise builder estimates the cost of a tower to be certain his funds match his vision. The parable is an admonition to count the cost of becoming His disciple—"joining the club" on an emotional whim is not going to get you through the difficult times. From this parable, we investors can glean the application that jumping in without commitment and knowledge can be equally disastrous.

The following questions will guide you as you inquire regarding ministry projects:

- What are the overall expectations of this project?
- How does this project fit the mission statement of the organization?
- Is another group engaged in a similar project; is there a duplication of effort/funding?
- Are there specific measurable goals and benchmarks for the project?
- Who will provide progress reports, and how often will he or she do so?
- How much of the project is presently funded?
- What faith challenges are evident beyond financial ones?
- Will the project become a self-sustaining, self-supporting entity?

Exerting the effort to investigate these matters will help to assure God's resources are not spent on mere good intentions but on projects that will have both earthly and eternal impact on the kingdom.

These six areas, if thoroughly researched, will translate your God-given passion into a giving experience that will bless the organization, the intended benefactors of the project, and you.

Paul's benediction to the generous Corinthians demonstrates the far-reaching ripples of their gifts:

> *This service that you perform is not only supplying the needs of God's people but is also overflowing in many expressions of thanks to God. Because of the service by which you have proved yourselves, men will praise God for the obedience that accompanies your confession of the gospel of Christ, and for your generosity in sharing with them and with everyone else. And in their prayers for you their hearts will go out to you, because of the surpassing grace God has given you. Thanks be to God for his indescribable gift!*
>
> —*2 Corinthians 9:12–15*

IPOs and Start-Ups

If ever there was a suspect start-up, this was it.

The small company was led by a CEO in absentia. There was no president, though several employee-volunteers had once expressed the desire to fill the slot. Few of them held advanced degrees, and the top brass averaged just three years of on-the-job training. Oh, and they were "employee-volunteers" because there were no hard or liquid assets with which to pay salaries. Their mission statement was certainly clear, but their strategy statement was sketchy at best. Decisions were often made on the fly, which worked well in the beginning, but this methodology was later marred by politics and infighting.

If you haven't guessed by now, this "company" was the church of Jerusalem, established AD 33 by the Lord Jesus Christ.

Rolled out as an IPO, this company wouldn't cause many to reach for their checkbook. Yet over the next few years its employees turned the world upside down—and today Christianity is the most widespread of any religion on the face of the earth.

We do not write this to contradict the many principles we've shared thus far, but we do want to offer this as a reminder that today's blue chips are not always large and hallowed establishments—and that today's blue chips weren't always so blue! With the changing face of American culture and world missions, there are many "baby blues" God is using to impact His world. Just because they may still be in the formative stages, that does not mean they get a pass on meeting the criteria outlined in the six aforementioned areas. If an organization truly aspires to do God's work in this age and culture, it will already have adopted many of the values, methods, and strategies practiced by their more-established counterparts.

As you search for your blue chips, don't just consult the "Fortune 500" of ministries and missions. It is not God's plan to consolidate His funds in the hands of a few, so don't forget to turn over a few stones as you do your research.

A Final Checkup

Looking at ministries in light of these criteria is meaningless unless you take a few moments to examine yourself, the investor.

Paul, in his writings to the churches in Philippi and Corinth, expressed the desire that any gift be to the benefit of receiver and giver alike. We've experienced that type of reciprocity in our lives, and we believe that this is the earthly part of the reward God gives us for doing as He desires.

While the receiver is always blessed, there are no guaranteed rewards for the giver (remember 1 Cor. 13:3). To prepare our own hearts, we have developed a set of questions to assure what we're doing is first and foremost for God's glory but also of earthly and lasting benefit to the receiver and to us.

HAVE WE INVESTED ENOUGH TIME ASKING GOD FOR HIS GUIDANCE PRIOR TO THIS INVESTMENT?

Prayer has been stressed every step of the way, and it is critical to seek God's peace before taking the final step. This does not guarantee that every investment will bear the fruit we or the organization hoped for, but it does guarantee that our participation in it is God's desire for us and our resources.

IS OUR MOTIVATION FOR GIVING PURE?

It's not hard to do the right thing for the wrong reason. It happens all too often in the Christian life, but we do want to guard against that. Giving with any tinge of pride, giving out of compulsion, giving in order to receive more in return—these are just a few of the attitudes that will negate the reward God means for us to experience.

HAVE WE DONE DUE DILIGENCE ANALYZING THIS ORGANIZATION?
At this point the question should almost be rhetorical in nature. Yet in the off chance we may have overlooked an area, or even dismissed a yellow light along the way, we like to take one more walk through our criteria. We want to be certain we have satisfied the criteria of the faithful steward—faithful with the things of another, and faithful even in the little things.

IS THIS ORGANIZATION AND PROJECT IN ALIGNMENT WITH OUR PERSONAL MISSION? IF NOT, WHY ARE WE CONSIDERING GIVING TO IT?
We believe that God has burdened our hearts with certain passions so we naturally give to organizations that have similar passions— but that doesn't mean we *only* give to organizations of like passion. We believe His Spirit can move us to give outside our primary realm of evangelism, and these questions help us to honestly evaluate why we are doing so.

IS THERE ANY CONFLICT OF INTEREST IN GIVING TO THIS ORGANIZATION?
If we have a vested interest (apart from kingdom interests) in the organization or could be accused (rightly or wrongly) of selecting it for reasons that could be considered questionable, this is a good point to stop and reevaluate. More than likely, if our hearts are in the right place from the beginning, this will be a nonissue. Still, it's an important part of the review process.

WHO WILL BE MY/OUR ACCOUNTABILITY PARTNERS?

When we give, we are making a commitment to God and to the organization, and though this commitment may not technically be binding in the court of law, it certainly is before God. That is why it's important to have that faithful person or persons in your life to help you follow through on your commitment. I have learned not to trust myself alone—the episode of holding back after our windfall profit year is a good example of why I don't. This is why I count on Carin as my closest and most trusted accountability partner. Without accountability, it is too easy to give in to fears or worries instead of trusting God's purpose in the challenges that stretch us. If you don't have an accountability partner or partners, seek them out today.

So we may boldly say: "the Lord is my helper; I will not fear. What can man do to me?"

—*Hebrews 13:6* NKJV

CHAPTER SEVEN

Radical Trust, Radical Faith

⌒

The tension was unbearable.

"It's really quite simple," the man began, eyes darting around the room nervously. "You are the one with the deep pockets ... so you're going to have to pay."

A heavy, unspoken "or else" hung in the air. I sat there stunned. The man before me was suddenly more of an enigma than ever. I had met him briefly right around the time that I was considering participation in a partnership—one focused on the mortgage side of the industry, an area we'd yet to explore.

The "Dream Team" was already in place. Several highly qualified and experienced businessmen with proven track records in the mortgage and marketing arena had come together like the last pieces to a puzzle. As a venture capitalist he was the one who had put together the funding for this new company. It seemed perfect—we were all evenly yoked—or so I thought.

Since I had limited knowledge of the mortgage business and had no time to devote to developing and managing a new business, my participation would be limited. I agreed to a 10-percent equity ownership piece in exchange for the eventual financial advising and consulting of the mortgage brokers who would soon affiliate with the new company.

Several months later I began to hear rumblings of mismanagement and overspending and before I knew it, there I sat that December afternoon facing a man who was threatening my life and the life of my family.

"Let's approach this logically," I said, attempting to hide my fear as I geared up to give the best business presentation ever known to man. "We need to handle this problem properly—using the court system. A strong case can be made that various people mishandled the seed money and justice would be served if we would patiently plead our case in court."

He sat across from me, expressionless. A tall thug of a man stood off to his side, a stoic bodyguard-looking type wearing a suit and dark sunglasses. "My investors won't wait. The 'family' wants their money within thirty days."

"The family? Who are your investors?" I finally asked, sensing I wasn't going to like his answer.

"That's not important," he said. "What's important is that we return all of the money that was spent to my source ... and fast."

And there it was again, another "or else."

Was he talking about organized crime?

"If we don't ... if *you* don't," he continued, "bad things will start happening to your family … really bad things…. We start with the children…."

Another Grisham novel? Sadly, no. This is a true story. There is much more to the story—though I won't go into those details here. But I wanted to tell you about this drama for a very important reason. It demonstrates yet another truth about becoming a faithful giver: Giving is not just a financial challenge, it's also a spiritual battle. Here was a man intent on extorting money from me through threats and coercion. Some of the very tools of the Prince of Darkness himself.

Now, before you think I'm going off the deep end here, I need to let you know I don't typically spiritualize things. I'm not quick to point to every event and say it's a direct result of some spiritual battle going on (though I certainly believe that is often true). But this one … this had the fingerprints of the Enemy all over it—the lies, the deception, the intent to steal our resources. And why wouldn't he want to attack us? We were enjoying yet another good year, which translated to significant dollars already invested in kingdom work and a year-end sum just waiting to join the previous monies.

I'm not going to pretend we weren't afraid. Carin and I initially struggled mightily over what to do. Should we hand over the money and hope that was the last we'd see of the extorter? Hope that his "source" would leave us alone? And then there were the uncertainties—where did he really get the money in the first place? Did he truly have connections to organized crime, or was he merely a brilliant con man?

Fear and doubt consumed us. As we considered going to the

authorities, we backpedaled, remembering that included in the threats was a "by the way—I have connections on the inside." But the battle was not one-sided. The Lord was right there with us. When we were at our wit's end and unable to make a decision He sent an "angel of light" in the uniform of a private security advisor. This man sat down on our sofa to help us discuss family security measures but promptly turned into one of God's workers. He informed us that he was a Christian and walked us through Scriptures and refreshed us with God's perspective on this matter. We also learned that the Lord had situated a prayer warrior in the office right above mine. We met him soon after this saga began and without knowing anything about the warfare we were experiencing he told us that he had been prompted to pray for the person in the office below him. He had even etched Scripture on the floor during the build-out phase of his office. We were covered and protected without even realizing it.

And then, we were given a final confirmation of who really was in charge of this battle. It was December and amidst the chaos we needed to go over those year-end numbers and figure out how much more we needed to give to the Lord's work based on the income of that year. We were stunned to discover that our extorter was asking for the exact amount of money that we calculated we needed to give at year-end.

Coincidence? I suppose someone might argue that. But the odds were certainly astronomically against it. This was no small sum. God was sending us a message: This is His money, meant for His purposes.

As Carin and I considered all this, we wrestled with what it might mean if we didn't pay the extorter—if we operated under the assumption that he was bluffing. But what if we were wrong? It could mean our lives, or worse—the lives of our children. It felt like we were living in a nightmare that would never end. And yet, somewhere in the midst of the turmoil we found peace … we were ready. If God were to call us home, we would have gone willingly, with the comfort of knowing that we were obedient to God's call on our lives—to steward and protect His resources so they will be used for His glory.

Sometimes we ask why Lord, why us? But the real question we should ask is why *not* us. We feel honored that He knew ahead of time that somehow we would be able to pass this test and that, in the end, He would be glorified. We have grown to appreciate these tests when they come for we trust that no test of faith would occur without our Father allowing it. His divine plan was to bring us to a new level of trust and purpose and for that lesson we are eternally grateful.

We all face difficulties and battles during our lives, but it is all about how we choose to respond. Will our faith stand the test? Will we encourage the faith of others by the way we respond? We have met many people that have become leaders in dealing with adversity. Here are just two.

After experiencing what must be the most painful experience in a parent's life, the loss of a child, Greg Laurie's life had suddenly taken a left-hand turn. We can only imagine how difficult it must be to attempt to recover from such a tragedy. Greg's loss of his thirty-three-year-old son, Christopher, happened just before the Harvest Crusade where Greg would deliver a message of hope and the love of Christ to thousands at Anaheim Stadium. Greg's comfort came in preaching the gospel not only to others but also to himself. Greg said, "Just saying those beautiful words of comfort from the Bible about where loved ones in the Lord go when they die encouraged me." Talk about a "radical faith" leaning on the love of our heavenly Father when inexplicable things happen! May we all be encouraged to deal with adversity as Greg Laurie has been and always remember to persevere and hold fast to our faith—no matter what.

In 1967 a young girl dove into the water and her life became changed forever. Joni Eareckson (later Tada) became a quadriplegic. Her life easily could have taken a different direction after the debilitating accident. She could have wallowed in self-pity. She could have played the victim and become bitter. Instead she leads an international ministry, Joni and Friends, a Christian outreach ministry to a disability community of 610 million people worldwide. Joni is a successful author, accomplished artist, gifted vocalist, and a strong voice for the rights of the disabled in our world. Joni is well acquainted with suffering and struggle, having spent over four decades confined to a wheelchair. And yet her praise to God is continuous and the love of Jesus permeates her very being. She once expressed gratefulness for her quadriplegic limitations because it allowed others to exercise *their* gifts of service. Through her writings, her art, her song, her speaking, and her ministry Joni is an example and role model for what can happen when we obediently live a life surrendered to a "radical faith."

In the end we didn't pay the extortionist. Instead we wrote the checks to the many ministries we supported that year, and we have never regretted our decision. We often think that the battle for the soul of someone, somewhere in the world was raging intensely during that time. Someday we will know the details. As difficult as that exercise was we remember the incredible and powerful ways God has already used us to make a difference in the world, and then consider all the ways He still intends to bring glory unto Himself as we continue to seek what it means to be faithful with much.

There is *much* work to be done so if you have been granted custody of resources that can be used to accomplish *much,* we challenge you to become radical in your faith and trust in our Lord. Don't let anything hold you back. You may be running the "lead-off leg"—as a leader, a visionary; or that all important "second leg" as a motivator, an implementer or encourager; or maybe even the "third leg" like us, passing the resources on to that all important "anchor" who will bring the message to the masses. Whatever position you have in the race, run hard and remember that your efforts will not go unrewarded.

> "His master replied, 'Well done, good and faithful servant! You have been faithful with a few things; I will put you in charge of many things. Come and share your master's happiness!'"
> —Matthew 25:21

Are you ready to trust God … with everything? Then we invite you to join us in breaking down the barriers to generous giving and to start giving with a radical trust and with a radical faith. We pray that you will seek Him diligently and discover a new and exciting way to make a difference in this world with His resources.

"Only hold on to what you can hold with an open hand."

The kingdom work awaits.

APPENDIX

Wealth Mission Statement

—

The following is meant to be an outline to help guide you through the process of creating your own wealth mission statement.

A. Start with an overall statement of purpose that includes …

- What is to be accomplished
- How is it to be accomplished
- Who will be the primary focus

For example it may look something like this …

Our purpose is to express our intentions regarding the distribution of our material assets. We have been blessed with more than we need to live out our expected lifetime. Our overall objective is to provide for our heirs and to various ministries we have chosen whose primary focus is evangelism. We will accomplish our goals by providing clear and specific directions by utilizing legal tools and strategies that will minimize tax implications and maximize our ultimate distribution. We desire to leave a lasting legacy and provide an example of generosity for our children that is not self-focused on accumulation but on impacting lives of those who are less fortunate.

B. Clarify values that reflect your beliefs and guide your decision making and actions which might include …

- Values and beliefs about who owns what and our stewardship responsibilities.
- Values and beliefs about giving and helping those less fortunate.
- Value of family and teaching generosity and service.
- Value of evangelism and the great commission at home and abroad.
- Value of honoring God and eternal rewards.

For example you might express your values like this …

We believe that God owns it all.

"'The silver is mine and the gold is mine,' declares the LORD Almighty." (Hag. 2:8)

We believe that we are stewards and are owners of second position.

"But remember the LORD your God, for it is he who gives you the ability to produce wealth." (Deut.8:18)

"Moreover, when God gives any man wealth and possessions ...this is a gift of God." (Ecc.5:19)

"The LORD sends poverty and wealth; he humbles and exalts." (1 Sam.2:7)

We believe God expects a return on His investment.

"Again, it will be like a man going on a journey, who called his servants and entrusted his property to them.... After a long time the master of those servants returned and settled accounts with them." (Matt. 25:14–19)

We believe God rewards the investment of our time, treasure, and talent.

"The man who had received the five talents brought the other five. 'Master,' he said, 'you entrusted me with five talents. See I have gained five more.' His master replied, 'Well done, good and faithful servant! You have been faithful with a few things; I will put you in charge of many things. Come and share your master's happiness.'" (Matt. 25:20–21)

C. Develop a brief overview of your philosophy and theology relative to money.

For example ...

Many of our attitudes are shaped by how our life is centered. We want to be countercultural to our world where the accumulation of money is often the end goal and a primary focus of our lives. Money to us is not the end goal but a means or a tool to be invested on behalf of bringing a return that is not self-centered and self-serving but advances God's agenda. The Bible is clear about the attitudes we should have relative to our money, our lifestyle, and our ambition.

"For the love of money is a root of all kinds of evil. Some people, eager for money, have wandered from the faith and pierced themselves with many griefs." (1 Tim. 6:10)

D. Wealth transfer and beneficiaries.

This section will provide specific guidelines that will guide the development of your will, trusts and other legal documents.

For example ...

Using our resources for God's glory during our lives has been our passion. It is our hope and prayer, that after our deaths, the legacy will continue through our family members and heirs. Specifically we challenge our children to carefully consider the responsibility that comes with the financial gift you will receive. You are now the torchbearer of God's financial resources—not yours—so pray for wisdom and guidance as to how you can continue the legacy of giving in our family. Many will be watching you. To our trustees that will work to distribute assets to ministries according to the terms in our trusts—be diligent, prayerful, and wise as you carry out your duties. Be a shining example to everyone you deal with and pray for the effectiveness of each gift before giving it.

"One man pretends to be rich, yet has nothing; another pretends to be poor, yet has great wealth." (Prov. 13:7)

"Do not wear yourself out to get rich; have the wisdom to show restraint." (Prov. 23:4)